POLYPORUS BETULINUS, A FUNGUS, GROWS ON A
PAPER BIRCH TREE IN THE ADIRONDACK MOUNTAINS.

Cheery fire blazes at the campsite of writer Chris Eckstrom Lee in the Adirondack Park, a backcountry area of private and public lands in upstate New York.

Prepared by the Special Publications Division
National Geographic Society
Washington, D. C.

*Exploring
America's*

Backcountry

Winter comes to desert mountains: December snow blankets shrubs high in Death Valley

EXPLORING AMERICA'S BACKCOUNTRY
Published by the National Geographic Society

Robert E. Doyle, *President*
Melvin M. Payne, *Chairman of the Board*
Gilbert M. Grosvenor, *Editor*
Melville Bell Grosvenor, *Editor Emeritus*

Prepared by the Special Publications Division

Robert L. Breeden, *Editor*
Donald J. Crump, *Associate Editor*
Philip B. Silcott, *Senior Editor*
Merrill Windsor, *Consulting Editor*

Ron Fisher, *Managing Editor*
Thomas B. Powell, III, *Picture Editor*
Jody Bolt, *Art Director*
Tom Melham, *Assistant to the Managing Editor*
Bonnie S. Lawrence, Barbara Grazzini, Kathleen F. Teter, *Research*

Illustrations and Design

Bonnie S. Lawrence, *Assistant to the Picture Editor*
Suez B. Kehl, *Assistant Art Director;* Turner Houston,
    Marianne Rigler Koszorus, Cinda Rose, *Design Assistants*
John Eastcott, Toni Eugene, Christine Eckstrom Lee,
    Tom Melham, Yva Momatiuk, H. Robert Morrison,

National Monument. Slopes of California's Panamint Range edge Harrisburg Flats.

Cynthia Russ Ramsay, Jennifer C. Urquhart,
Suzanne Venino, *Picture Legends*

John D. Garst, Jr., Susanah B. Brown, George E. Costantino,
Margaret Deane Gray, Dewey G. Hicks, Jr.,
Map Research, Design, and Production

Engraving, Printing, and Product Manufacture
Robert W. Messer, *Manager*
George V. White, *Production Manager*
June L. Graham, Richard A. McClure, Raja D. Murshed,
Christine A. Roberts, *Assistant Production Managers*
David V. Showers, *Production Assistant*

Debra A. Antonini, Barbara Bricks,
Jane H. Buxton, Rosamund Garner,
Suzanne J. Jacobson, Amy E. Metcalfe,
Cleo Petroff, Katheryn M. Slocum,
Suzanne Venino, *Staff Assistants*

Martha K. Hightower,
Brit Aabakken Peterson, *Index*

*S*watch of sun-tinted pink ripples among ghostly cypress stumps in the Upper Flat lake, a body of water

in the Atchafalaya swamp of southern Louisiana.

Sawtooth Range

Azure Lakes and Rocky Trails: Camping and Climbing in Idaho

By Constance Brown
Photographs by Paul Chesley

With some amusement, I recalled a perplexing statement I'd read in a U. S. Forest Service publication that described the brisk parade of seasons in the Sawtooth Range of central Idaho. "Spring comes in early July," it said, "and the fall season starts in August." "Then when is summer?" I wondered. I was peering down on the shoreline of mile-long Sawtooth Lake on a Saturday morning in early August. Lying prone, propped on my elbows, I gazed at the largest and perhaps the most beautiful of the three hundred lakes and ponds in the 216,383-acre Sawtooth Wilderness. The sky was a cloudless blue, the lake a dark sapphire. A long slab of snow hugged the shaded southern shore beneath 10,190-foot Mount Regan, but the water was free of ice.

I rolled over and sat up facing the rocky peak. With binoculars I scanned the cliffs for mountain goats. About three hundred of the shaggy, cantankerous creatures are known to inhabit the range; so far, not one had revealed itself to me. Only whitebark pines, like solitary sentinels, came into focus. Each stunted, twisted tree stood separate, an individual survivor of past winters.

I put away my binoculars and picked up a hand magnifier. The tiny white blossoms in a clump of pussytoes beside me ballooned to twice their size. Around me, a profusion of color accented the sparse mountain grasses growing at 8,400 feet: scarlet Indian paintbrush, red-and-yellow columbine, pink mountain laurel. Water flowed gently from a small lake above me down into Sawtooth Lake. A thousand buttercups grew in its marshy channel. They shimmered in the breeze, dancing.

"Summer is right now," I concluded.

This was one of the most peaceful—and languorous—days I'd spent in more than a month of exploring the sparsely forested, dramatically glaciated peaks and valleys of the Sawtooth Range with photographer Paul

July snow blankets a trail in central Idaho's Sawtooth Range as Jan Meeks, off-duty wilderness ranger, and her part-Samoyed dog, Kelly, romp through drifts near Sand Mountain Pass. Spring comes late to this high country.

Chesley. The mountains are a part of the Sawtooth Wilderness, which is located in the western part of the Sawtooth National Recreation Area.

We had determined to see as much of the backcountry as possible during the short warm season, in a dozen forays on foot and horseback. Sometimes we explored alone. At other times we enjoyed the camaraderie of mountaineers and rock-climbers, of rangers, ranchers, and miners, of horse packers and friends.

Three hundred miles of trails crisscross the compact 32-by-18-mile range. Most climb the glacial troughs that slope down between the peaks, but Paul and I often hiked off the trails to see the real backcountry. It was like walking along the pleated bellows of an accordion: up, down, up, down. Distances were short, elevations great, and the scenic rewards were often spectacular. On one trip, we found Shangri-La.

That's what rock-climbers call a secluded hanging valley near Redfish Lake that provides excellent climbing. Hanging valleys are common in the area. They occur where a tributary glacier once entered a trunk glacier from the side. The side valley isn't gouged as deeply as the main valley. Often a waterfall plummets from the hanging valley.

Paul and I were on a three-day outing with rock-climbers Bob Rosso, Kevin Swigert, and Mark Siemon, all Idaho residents. It was raining and misty as we ascended 1,600 feet along the steep and slippery bank of a stream, through a notch, to a campsite in a stand of pine trees between two small lakes. The Elephants Perch, a massive granite face, loomed 2,000 feet above the camp. Bob and Kevin planned to climb a 600-foot pinnacle on its flank—the Elephants Tusk—the next day.

After setting up camp, we explored the valley and climbed the talus below one of the summits. "There's a lot of good climbing in the Sawtooths," Kevin told me. "But you have to spend quite a bit of time hiking to it. It's not like at Yosemite, where you can drive up to a cliff and climb practically off the top of your car."

Both 23-year-old Kevin and 19-year-old Mark have been members of U. S. Nordic ski teams—and hope to be again. They climb primarily for relaxation from their rigorous summer ski-training program. They run an average of 120 miles a month, often following Sawtooth trails.

The August rain continued and turned to snow that night. We huddled around our campfire, drying socks and other gear, and talked about the sport the climbers love so much. "I think climbing will always remain a sport of the few," Bob said. "Not because it's dangerous—it's exceedingly safe once you master the technical skills—but because it's so strenuous."

The next morning I watched from an adjacent cliff as the pair scaled the cold, damp granite of the Tusk. Kevin, who conditions himself constantly, moved up fluidly. Not so Bob, who owns a busy sporting-goods shop in Ketchum and is prone to a familiar workingman's problem: lack of spare time to train and climb.

Some 400 feet up the wall, Bob dramatically illustrated how strenuous climbing can be. Halted at a vertical slab, he groped for ten minutes trying to find hand- and footholds. A hollow silence stretched between us. I could not aid him in his search. His legs were visibly shaking as, with ebbing strength, he gripped the wall.

Finally he moved, pulling himself up past the difficult spot. "It's getting harder every year to step out of the shop and onto a rock face," he called, relief in his voice. Sierra, his Labrador retriever, stalled in confusion at the base of the cliff, howled when she heard Bob's shout.

The Forest Service frequently warns the backpackers who hike the Sawtooth trails that this is not the place to make their first attempt at

An arm of the Rocky Mountains, the 32-mile-long Sawtooth Range embraces jagged peaks, flowered meadows, and alpine lakes. The Salmon River rises east of the mountains, beckoning fishermen and rafters; from Sawtooth Valley to the White Cloud Peaks, livestock graze rich pastures. In 1972, a Congress mindful of the aesthetic and recreational values of the region established the 754,000-acre

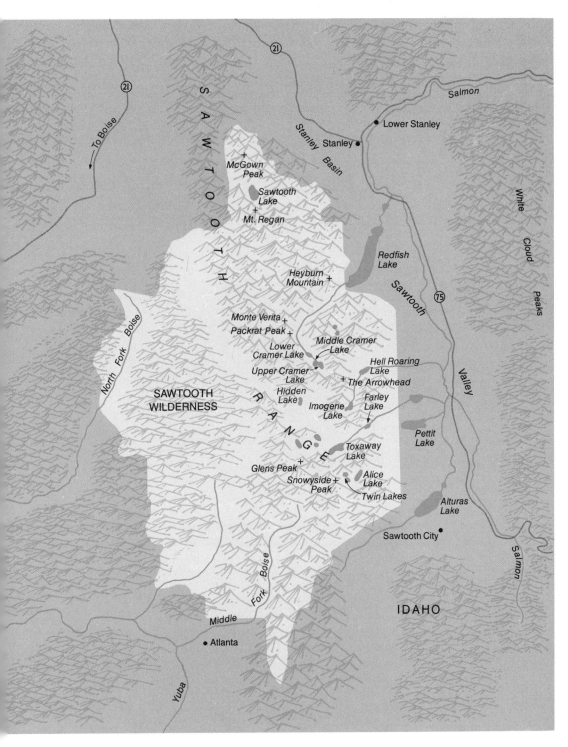

Sawtooth National Recreation Area and designated the western third of that—the range—as the Sawtooth Wilderness.

scaling a convenient rock face. Still, a few fatal accidents have occurred. "You have to know where it's safe to climb, because in many areas the rock crumbles and cracks in your hand—like stale bread," a climber told me. "It's weathering rapidly, by geological standards."

Before leaving Shangri-La, Mark led me up an easier route to the summit of the Elephants Perch. To the north stood Heyburn Mountain, a perfect example of weathered rock. Its crumbly summit has eroded to resemble a Gothic cathedral, complete with buttresses and spires.

Heyburn appeared to be about the same elevation as the surrounding peaks. There are 16 named mountains in the range that stand more than 10,000 feet high; yet none surpasses 10,751 feet. Later I found out why.

The Sawtooth Range, according to some geologists, was formed along fault zones in the earth's crust. Batholiths, layers of igneous rock that rose from the molten depths millions of years ago, underlie the Sawtooth area, and—like blisters under the skin—have caused severe pressure on the land's surface.

During the last 30 million years, several long faults have slowly ruptured the surface, relieving some of the pressure.

Between two of the main faults, a block of granite emerged—a giant massif that tilted a bit to the northeast, like a floating crate. It eventually rose to more than 10,000 feet.

Simultaneously, rivers and other forces of erosion, plus gargantuan alpine glaciers during the Pleistocene Epoch beginning some two million years ago, started sculpturing the mountains we see today. Their summits, naturally, can never be higher than the original massif, and most retain its approximate elevation.

Hundreds of lakes lie among the peaks in cirques, amphitheater-like bowls dug out at the heads of glacial valleys. Others are dammed behind moraines, enormous piles of rocky sediments deposited by melting glaciers. Some glacial moraines reach far into Stanley Basin and the Sawtooth Valley. Forested with tough lodgepole pines, which thrive in the porous soil, they are the foothills of the Sawtooths.

From the air, many groups of Sawtooth lakes appear to be strung out like beads, one below the other. Called paternoster lakes, after the rosary that Roman Catholics use in prayer, they were created in sequence by the glaciers that crept down the valleys, some as recently as 8,000 years ago. The three Cramer lakes, southwest of Redfish Lake, form a perfect paternoster pattern. One cloudless Sunday afternoon they were the site of a gourmet picnic that Paul and I are not likely to forget.

Connie Maricich had arranged the outing. She often quits her Sun Valley boutique to backpack into the mountains with friends, where they share elaborate, precooked picnics. She has compiled a delightful cookbook on the subject, *The Picnic Gourmet.*

Laden with exotic provisions, all carefully stored in our backpacks, six of us trudged along the seven-mile trail to Upper Cramer Lake. Connie's friend Pierre Chesnel, an amusing, cheerful Frenchman, carried several bottles of wine, in addition to a roast chicken stuffed with veal and mushroom paté. "If I get lost, I have everything I need," he quipped.

We arrived at the lake in time for a quick swim to rinse off the trail dust, then chose a grassy hummock between two shallow, snowmelt rivulets for our picnic site. The hummock was speckled with pink and yellow wild flowers, but also seemed to be a popular feeding ground for a ravenous regiment of enormous Sawtooth mosquitoes.

The 2,000-foot valley wall behind us formed an amphitheater that caught the last rays of afternoon sunshine (Continued on page 29)

Wilderness Ranger Jan Meeks, a roving ambassador, talks with three backpackers on the Alice Lake Trail. During five-day patrols in the Sawtooth Wilderness, Jan explains regulations, grades and digs out trails, cleans fire pits, and reminds hikers to pack out their litter.

"**Y**ou get hooked on this country," says Jan of her work as a ranger. "Every day when I wake up and go out, I'm amazed. It changes all the time." Hungry and hopeful, Kelly eyes a fellow hiker's candy bar while he and Jan rest near Toxaway Lake. To keep trails clear, Jan saws and removes dead timber (right). Toppled by heavy snows, a 20-foot alpine fir blocks the path from the lake. "My kind of job draws people who like being out in the wilderness, enjoy being alone, and don't mind hard work," Jan says. Seven rangers, three of them women, work all summer to maintain the Sawtooth Wilderness.

FOLLOWING PAGES: *Streamers of snow drape granite slopes hemming Alice Lake. Its beauty and accessibility attract more than 3,000 visitors to this glacier-gouged lake each year, making the area one of the most heavily used in the range.*

*S*unshine and shadow dapple the trail as brother-and-sister outfitters Jeff and Sally Bitton hoist a 75-pound bundle of equipment onto a packhorse near Edna Lake. They guided the Irwin family of Yakima, Washington, on a four-day pack trip in the eastern Sawtooths. Morning at camp includes sharing a mirror: Deanna smears on insect repellent while Wendy brushes her hair (opposite, above). Jeff, the breakfast chef, browns sourdough hotcakes. Stumbling over granite boulders, the campers clamber down the flank of Glens Peak.

FOLLOWING PAGES: Homeward bound with Jeff in the lead, the packtrain picks its way along a path above Toxaway Lake.

19

*S*pring snows yield to a meadow of lavender
beardtongue and scarlet Indian paintbrush on
the shore of Sawtooth Lake. Multitudes of wild
flowers tint these hillsides in July and August.
At right, a Pieris butterfly an inch and a half
wide alights on the vivid bracts of an Indian
paintbrush. Rosy half-inch blooms of mountain
laurel spill from a stone crevice on Toxaway
Trail (left); white blossoms of an herb of the
phlox family carpet rocky heights.

*S*unlight warms
rumpled crags in the
northern Sawtooths.
Hewn from one
huge massif, 16
named peaks in the
range reach skyward
more than 10,000
feet; the tallest soars
to 10,751. Popular
with climbers, The
Arrowhead (below)
juts like a prehistoric
megalith some 70 feet
above a ridge west of
Hell Roaring Lake.

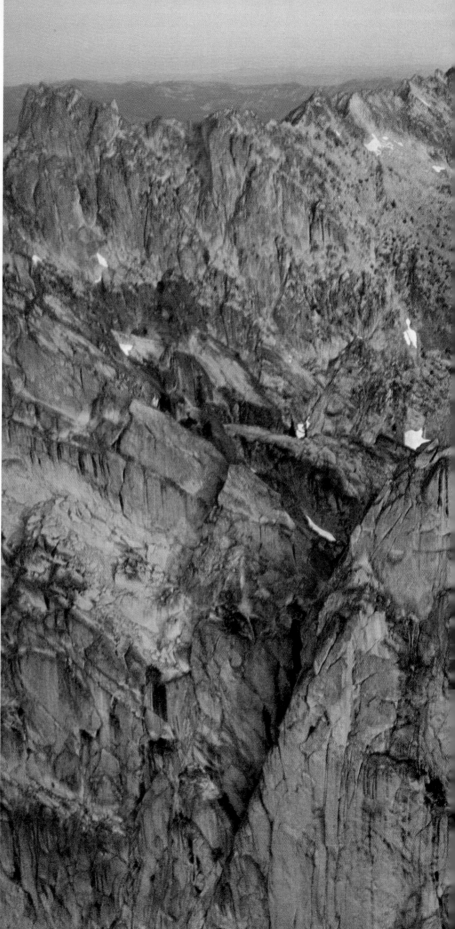

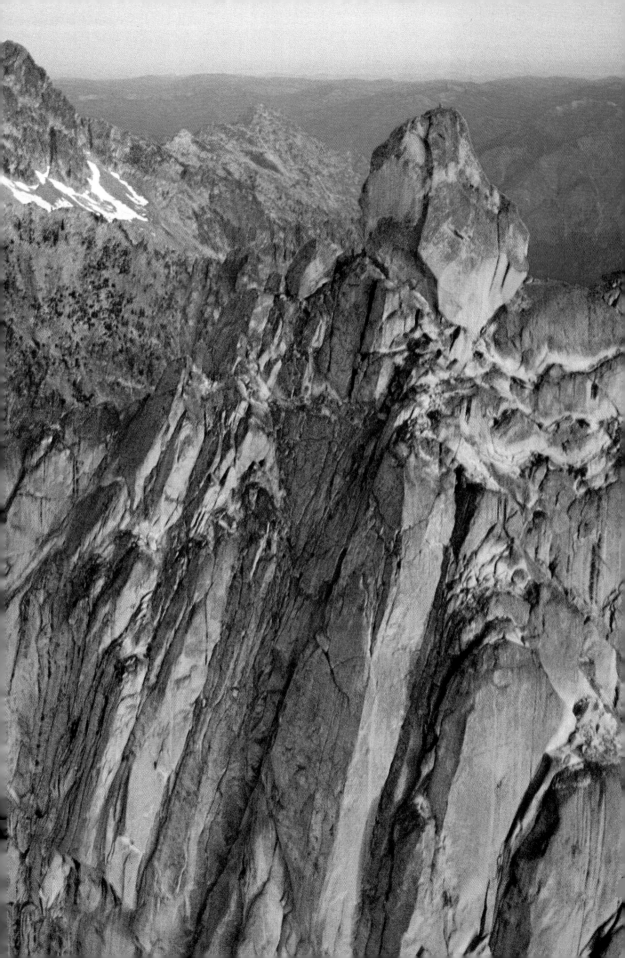

Canopy of clouds drifts to the horizon as author Constance Brown pitches her tent beside a rocky pool. The White Cloud Peaks rise in the distance. Beneath The Arrowhead's looming wedge (right), Connie and photographer Paul Chesley combine corned beef, fresh mushrooms, zucchini, onions, and powdered sour cream to create beef Stroganoff. At 9,000 feet, perennial snowfields cling to the slopes behind their campsite. Harsh winters and short growing seasons deter most animal residents, but some live here all year. A chubby pika emerges from its lichen-encrusted den. Whistling as they work, these seven-inch relatives of rabbits—nicknamed "haymakers"—gather and stockpile grasses and herbs all summer. The haystacks, some as big as a bushel basket, sustain the animals through the cold months. Rugged terrain discouraged exploration in the Sawtooths. Fur hunter Alexander Ross reached the range in 1824 and described the Indians he found there, but not until after the Idaho gold rush of the 1860's did settlers move into the Sawtooth Valley.

27

and bounced them onto us. On top, an impressive rock formation called The Arrowhead reached another 70 feet or so into the sky. Wider in the middle than at its base or top, it looks like a crudely fashioned hunting point. It is a remnant of a much higher ridgetop; all the rock around it has long since eroded away.

Plates and containers of French mustard, homemade chutney, imported goat cheeses, salad dressings, and such delicacies as eggs stuffed with caviar soon covered the batik picnic cloths. Connie orchestrated the meal. I stirred an artichoke and leek soup over a backpacking stove. Pierre washed watercress and basil in the stream, and set it on the bank to dry.

Two more friends arrived, contributing Italian eggplant pie and plum upside-down cake. We commenced our feast, and even the aroma of insect repellent couldn't detract from its flavor. When we returned to the roadhead the next day, our packs were considerably lighter.

In the middle of the Sawtooth National Recreation Area are Stanley Basin and the Sawtooth Valley. They combine to provide a pastoral buffer zone fronting the majestic Sawtooth escarpment—a lyric time warp from the early part of this century, when 160-acre homestead ranches were the basis of a largely agricultural economy. Cattle graze knee-deep in fragrant pastures. Zigzag lodgepole fences snake between meadows rich with wild flowers, where horses run. Sandhill cranes nest near bleating sheep, and rutted dirt roads end at low-slung log cabins.

Regulations governing the use of the 25,000 acres of private land in the recreation area severely restrict development, thus preserving the rustic western atmosphere and the pastoral view of the Sawtooths. The regulations also control renovation and construction in the area's three tiny communities: Sawtooth City, Stanley, and Lower Stanley.

At six o'clock one morning I stood beside a weathered corral in a dew-soaked meadow in Sawtooth Valley and watched Busterback Ranch partner Jay Sevy and his crew of cowboys load several hundred fat cattle into livestock trucks. The early-morning cool and damp kept down the flies and dust. The quiet of the morning was broken by the jarring racket of hooves pounding on the trucks' aluminum decks.

The Busterback is Sawtooth Valley's second largest ranch, and one of its most beautiful. It was created in part from four original homesteads, and lots of "bust-your-back" work. The Forest Service has purchased scenic easements across much of its acreage.

"Essentially, what that means to us ranchers is that we can't subdivide," Jay explained as we toured the ranch after the cattle were loaded. "That's fine with us, since we didn't have any desire to do that in the first place, and the language in the easement is such that nobody can tell us how to go about our ranching."

North of Sawtooth Valley is Stanley Basin, where until recently thousands of sheep were pastured on federal lands. Basque and Peruvian herders, living in picturesque wooden camp wagons hitched behind their pickups or teams, tended the herds.

I was glad to know that regulations prevent the area from exploding with developments. Instead, a slice of the old agrarian West is perpetually preserved, complete with sheep and shepherds, cattle and cowboys.

The Salmon River originates in the mountains around Sawtooth Valley. Paul and I could see it shining silver in the afternoon sun from atop

Like beads on a string, the Cramer Lakes garland a woodland basin near Monte Verita and Packrat peaks. Glaciers carved these and other pools in rows, and they derive their geological name—paternoster lakes—from the rosary they resemble.

almost any peak at the edge of the valley. On one trip, we enjoyed the view from horseback. We joined Shirley and Jack Irwin, from Yakima, Washington, and their three young daughters—Leslie, Wendy, and Deanna—on a four-day pack trip with Jeff and Sally Bitton, brother-and-sister outfitters and guides.

We rode for 14 miles from Pettit Lake, through a few persistent snowdrifts on Sand Mountain Pass, to a campsite on the southern end of Edna Lake. The next morning, unencumbered by the pack string, which tended to pile up like a derailed train if we slowed on a switchback, we rode six more miles to Ardeth Lake and up a precipitous pass.

Twisted by stiff stirrups, my knees soon felt as if they were in a vise, and my rear end was numb. Nevertheless, the experience recalled happy memories. Two decades before, I'd spent several summers balanced astride surefooted ponies, exploring areas between Santa Fe and the Black Hills.

Dismounting, we tied our horses securely to sturdy whitebark pines and hiked toward Glens Peak. We were crossing a felsenmeer, or sea of rocks, and I felt as if we were on a pile of quarried granite. There wasn't a solid side to the peak, only angular boulders that had fallen in a heap, shorn from the bedrock during centuries of weathering.

At the summit, we turned on our heels in dizzying circles, taking in the spectacular view. Mountains rolled away in three directions, and bumped into bulbous cloud banks on the horizon. "I've counted 50 lakes below some summits," Jeff boasted. He swept his arm in a wide arc, pointing and counting until he came full circle with a total of 36.

Our 24-year-old guide was duplicating a lake-counting game first played by such Sawtooth guides as Dave Williams, who often led fishing and goat-hunting parties into the backcountry in the twenties and thirties. The guides not only counted Sawtooth lakes, but also named many of them for friends and relatives. Today those lakes recall another generation: Imogene, Alice, Edna, Farley, Vernon.

Williams led the first mountain climbers into the Sawtooths in 1934. While they donned climbing gear, he slipped into tennis shoes. When the going got really rough, he simply pulled off his shoes and climbed alongside them in his socks, sticking to the rocks like a mountain goat.

Back then, there weren't many trails in the range, and those that existed ran almost straight up the mountainsides, either for quick access to forest fires or for use by surveying teams. Leading us back to camp along such a trail, Jeff called over his shoulder, "This is how nearly all the trails used to be. Newer ones are better graded and a lot safer." We were climbing a contorted string of tight switchbacks. My horse's reins were lathered by his sweating neck. I shifted my weight forward to help him climb. "Trails nowadays are angled up more gradually to lessen erosion, and to make climbing easier," Jeff said. "But they aren't nearly as dramatic."

The packhorses welcomed us back to camp with loud whinnies. Wearily we unsaddled our mounts and headed for a dinner of grilled salmon steaks. As dusk fell, Deanna and Wendy perched like mermaids on a rock rising out of the lake. Jack pulled out his spinning rod and headed for the shore. When he returned a while later, happy but empty-handed, Jeff explained why the Sawtooth's lakes and streams don't support many trophy-size fish. "For one thing, Sawtooth waters are underlain largely by granite, which supplies few nutrients for the fish. For another, the growing season is short, because of the long cold winters. And finally, the most accessible lakes are heavily fished." We learned that the area doesn't support much wildlife, either—again because of the severe winters. "Except for mountain goats and small mammals, such as marmots and squirrels, not many animals can survive here all year, though some mule deer and elk migrate back and forth through the area."

Just then, as if to illustrate his point, a doe gingerly walked past the outskirts of our camp. We watched her intently. She was delicate and nimble, grazing on new green shoots sprouting from the moist soil.

The steady sound of splitting wood awakened me the next morning, and I lounged a few extra minutes in my tent, relishing my liberation from cooking and fire tending. I knew that Shirley was doing the same.

When I emerged, shafts of sunlight streaked the shaded camp, and the lake was very still. Jeff was flipping sourdough hotcakes on a griddle over the fire. Eggs were crackling in bacon grease alongside. A coffeepot nestled in the coals. I could gladly have loafed around the camp all day.

Instead, we headed for Hidden Lake, two hours north. After exploring the long, narrow lake and the steep pass beyond it, we let the horses graze in the high meadow while we lolled about in small groups on the fragrant earth, snoozing and sunning.

"Stop! Stop!" Deanna's sudden cries made me sit up. Somehow all of the horses except Jeff's had grouped and were trotting toward a pass, reins tied loosely to the saddle horns, stirrups flapping. We gave chase and, sensing our panic, they broke into a gallop. One of the girls managed to turn them, and they circled back toward us as the mountainside steepened. "Don't let them by or we'll be walking for sure," someone shouted.

Jeff saved the day. Mounting up, he cut the leaders out of the pack, and the remaining horses dispersed and slowed, like toys running down. One by one, we rounded them up. If they had run down the trail instead of circling back, they probably would have headed back to the ranch. "Horses can think," someone said, "but luckily for us they still can't reason." I, for one, was happy to have my irrational mount firmly beneath me as we headed back to the trail head at Pettit Lake the next afternoon.

Under the provisions of the Wilderness Act, the Sawtooths will continue to provide opportunities for solitude and the enjoyment of natural terrain. Sadly, everywhere Paul and I traveled, on and off the trails, we found evidence of overuse: trampled campsites; animal and human waste; litter; blackened campfire rings, often several within a few feet of each other; even, occasionally, live trees that had been cut for firewood.

Nearly everyone agrees that the Sawtooth Wilderness is fast becoming the worse for wear. Most wilderness areas in the country are partially protected from overuse by their remote locations. But the Sawtooth area is easily accessible. Its boundaries reach to within a mile of several roadheads. More than 21,000 people entered it in the summer of 1979.

The Sawtooths are too tall to hide and too scenic to ignore, so the Forest Service has developed a management plan that attempts to protect the fragile environment from too much use. Wilderness Zone Manager Dave Lee—the rusty-haired grandson of guide Dave Williams—discussed some of the problems and possible solutions with us when we visited his ranger station in Sawtooth Valley.

"For one thing, I sometimes wish there weren't any lakes in the Sawtooths," he said. "People seem to need a destination, and they invariably pick a lake. Lakes aren't hard to find; they stick out like jewels," he continued, pointing to a wall map. Thick black lines stretched between the lakes, delineating heavy traffic. "It results in overuse of the corridors between the most accessible lakes, and in heavy impact around them.

"We may have to require a permit for everyone entering the wilderness," he continued, "so we can distribute people more widely. And campfire bans around all the lakes may go into effect soon."

Dave knows, however, that the protection of the Sawtooth Range ultimately depends on the efforts of the many people who come to visit.

Jan Meeks knows it, too. She is one of seven wilderness rangers who work for Dave each summer, patrolling the most popular areas. She explains policies to hikers, maintains trails, and constantly cleans up after careless campers. Paul and I backpacked with her for five days along the heavily used trail that connects Pettit, Alice, Twin, and Toxaway lakes.

Jan has the tanned complexion and healthy good looks that result from spending a lot of time outdoors. At five feet seven inches, she seems dwarfed by the gear she carries. With shovel and trash bag in hand, and a three-foot bow saw and two-way radio lashed to her red backpack, she led the way up the trail. Her canine companion, a six-year-old part-Samoyed named Kelly, followed along.

The hillsides were covered with knee-high arrowleaf balsamroot, a kind of sunflower. White valerian grew along stream beds, where we often stopped to refresh ourselves as we trudged up the dusty trail. Jan identified two deep-pink flowering plants I saw in the moist soil: stalks of tiny elephanthead, and delicate, drooping blossoms of the shooting star.

"One of the delightful things about mountains," she said, "is that as you climb, you go back in time toward spring. While late-July flowers are blooming in the flatlands, early-June flowers are in bloom in the high meadows. That's why you saw buttercups at Sawtooth Lake in mid-August; they were blossoming in the lowlands two months earlier."

But rangers such as Jan do more than identify flowers for bewildered botanists like me. They may well be the Forest Service's most effective means of educating wilderness visitors.

"Hello there," Jan said cheerily, introducing herself to the first hiker we met. After chatting with him a few minutes, she prodded gently: "Are you using a backpacking stove for your cooking? We have a problem up here with too many campfires and not enough wood, so we're encouraging the use of stoves."

Like a professional lobbyist, Jan talked on any number of subjects with more than 75 people we encountered in the next few days, always managing to bend the conversation around to a discussion of camping skills that do not harm the environment.

"People don't mean to do this damage," she often said, most likely to remind herself, as she dismantled fire pits and shoveled up trash. "They just don't know any better."

"I am an aficionado of the area," she said to me at one point. "I *insist* everyone love it as much as I do."

On our last evening with Jan, we created a farewell chowder with our remaining provisions, all set out on a huge flat rock that sloped down and disappeared beneath the surface of Toxaway Lake. Huddled against a stiff breeze, we lit our stoves and combined fresh onions and zucchini with noodles, canned salmon, chicken bouillon, soy sauce, powdered milk, and spices. Jan's kitchen-grown alfalfa sprouts served as a salad.

After dinner, Jan sat beside her tent, recording notes in a log. Paul went for a hike, and I reclined on the rock, like an overfed marmot before the first snow. Across Sawtooth Valley, on the eastern horizon, the last rays of sunlight toasted distant pastel summits. The sky was pink, and it made the surface of the mile-long lake pink, too. No one was in sight along the shore. I had no chores to complete, no worries, no obligations to meet. Silence hummed in my ears. I closed my eyes and drifted off, experiencing the splendid peace of wilderness.

It is ironic that the Sawtooths are so popular today; 150 years ago nearly everyone except small bands of nomadic Sheepeater Indians chose to avoid them. The first white men to visit them were Alexander Ross and fellow trappers from the Hudson's Bay Company in 1824. But the steep, tumbling streams held little promise of beaver, so the mountains remained largely unexplored until the Civil War, when gold strikes north of the Sawtooths brought prospectors into the region. Boise became the capital of the Idaho Territory in 1864. That same year a small party of miners led by John Stanley came to what was later named Stanley Basin. They did some prospecting there, then some of the men headed southwest, through the Sawtooth Range.

They found placer gold on the Middle Fork of the Boise River. The news attracted droves of miners, and that fall a rich lode was discovered. Confederate sympathizers in the camp named it the Atlanta Lode, for Lt. Gen. John Hood's encounter with Maj. Gen. William T. Sherman in the 1864 battle of Atlanta—and the name stuck.

Mineral discoveries surrounded the Sawtooths during the next 15 years. But Atlanta was ultimately one of Idaho's most important gold-mining districts. Large-scale operations ended there in the mid-1950's when the Talache mining company shut down its mine and mill. Today Atlanta is a southern trail head into the Sawtooths, a summer retreat for Boise residents, and home to a few year-round miners and saloonkeepers.

Shorty Seaton came to Atlanta from an Iowa farm in 1937. He's one of the last hard-rock miners working here. Paul and I visited him at his one-room cabin three miles up a narrow, rutted road on the Yuba River. Showing us around his place, Shorty recollected his days in mining. "I did some placer mining, but there was no money in it. I worked for wages at the big mines in town, too. I've located three veins in my own Golden Stringer Mine," he said, smiling proudly. "The best one was two feet wide in some places. I worked it for 14 years. The one I'm working now is only one to four inches wide—but it's the purest gold I've ever found."

Shorty fixed lunch for us in his cabin. His bed was at one end of the narrow room, angled in front of a wood-burning stove. Provisions were tucked everywhere; a violin was propped in one corner; magazines were piled high. I imagined how cozy the room would be in winter, lit by butane lamps and warmed by the fire.

"Pretty soon there aren't going to be any prospectors left," Shorty predicted. "The government is what's making it difficult nowadays, passing all these pollution and safety laws. I do all my own work," he explained. "But I have to abide by laws made for the big companies. It's expensive."

Paul asked Shorty to play his violin for us. We stepped outside, and Shorty stood on the stoop in front of the screen door. Next to him, a rose bush bowed under the weight of dozens of yellow blossoms. Soft, lilting renditions of "Turkey in the Straw," "Irish Washerwoman," and "It's a Long Way to Tipperary" filled the air. I wanted to stay and listen, but it was time to say goodbye.

While Atlanta grew as a mining town, Stanley, just north of Sawtooth Valley, developed into a tourist center and a business hub for the surrounding mining camps and ranches. Situated at the crossroads of highways connecting Ketchum, Challis, and Boise, Stanley is a northern gateway to the entire recreation area, and field headquarters for several kayaking and rafting outfitters who conduct trips on the Salmon River and its middle fork.

Stanley's fabled Saturday Night Stomp is a top attraction for visitors. A couple of noisy, rustic bars feature country music and western dancing—a sort of jitterbugging that some say is harder work than hiking.

Another kind of dance—maneuvering on snow in crampons—prompted some advice from Lou Florence, owner of a mountaineering shop in Boise. "Walk like a bear," he said. "Put your full foot down, and keep your weight evenly distributed." I strapped the spiked metal extenders to my boots and took a few heavy, wide-set steps. It wasn't as difficult as I'd imagined. Five of us stood at the base of a snow couloir, or chute, 1,300 feet high near the summit of McGown Peak, west of Stanley. The couloir snaked down McGown's north face, reminding me of a drafty elevator shaft. But I wanted to climb it.

We'd left base camp before dawn, carrying lights to find our way through the lodgepole pines, junipers, and thick alder brush. It was a difficult trek. Then we negotiated several hundred feet of snow-covered talus slope to reach the base of the couloir.

Lou had explained why an early start was essential. "We want to hit it early, so the rocks that are frozen in the snow won't be loosened by the sun and fall down the chute onto us."

We began the ascent. Bob Henry, a Boise college student and accomplished climber, led Paul and me on one rope; Walt Henderson and Lou followed on another. With a cautious but determined momentum we worked our way up the shaded, frigid corridor, moving diagonally from one side to the other. The snow had melted away from the edges of the couloir, exposing pockets where we found safe, almost cozy ledges. Bob aimed for them, sometimes climbing almost to the end of the 150-foot rope that connected us.

When Bob had reached a ledge and secured the rope, Paul followed, climbing along the taut line. He was attached to it by a cord with a prussik, a forward-moving slipknot that would contract and hold if he fell backward. When he was secure next to Bob, I followed. As I climbed, Bob took up the slack in the rope.

I lost track of how many times we repeated the sequence—ten, maybe eleven. We were still climbing after five hours. The afternoon sun began hitting the top of the couloir, melting the snow.

I knew a falling rock could smash into a climber as he worked his way up the slope. I froze at the sound of a rattling above us. "Rock! Rock!" we shouted, to warn the climbers below. Several times projectiles bounded down the chute, but they bounced harmlessly off the snow or our helmets, injuring no one. I was a little frightened and eager to reach the top. The ledges where we rested were now thin and exposed, and the pitch of the snow was nearly 70 degrees. If I looked down the chute, vertigo made me sway. My breathing was uneven and rasping.

As I negotiated the last pitch, a large bird—a hawk, perhaps—passed silently overhead. It cast an enormous, elongated shadow across the sunlit couloir. Heartened, I felt my courage soar with it. I dug my ice ax into the soft snow and completed the last moves.

Perched safely at the summit of McGown, I was in a proud, expansive mood. Not because I had conquered a mountain, but because I had extended myself and succeeded. The mountain had lifted me up to share its magnificent view. A chill wind was blowing in my face, and the entire Sawtooth Range lay rough-and-tumble before me: a sea of storm-tossed granite. Protected forever as a wilderness area, it promised infinite challenges for future explorers like me. "Raw wilderness gives definition and meaning to the human enterprise," wrote conservationist Aldo Leopold.

Sitting triumphant at the summit of McGown, I heartily agreed.

Canine backpackers Targa and Sierra trudge up Redfish Lake Trail behind Bob Rosso, Mark Siemon, and Kevin Swigert. The dogs carried their own food when they joined their rock-climbing masters for a three-day trip into the Sawtooths.

*R*eflecting the pines and peaks that ring it, one of the Saddleback Lakes lures man and beast: Kevin Swigert casts as Sierra observes. Granite underlies most Sawtooth lakes and streams; water flowing over it picks up little in the way of nutrients, and thus supports few large fish. A short growing season and cold water also limit the size of the fish. In two hours, Kevin hooked only four seven-inch brook trout. Skewered on a limb, the first of his catch hangs beyond Sierra's reach. Kevin packed the fish into a camp pot (far left), then marinated them in lemon and herb sauce before the hikers devoured them. Patient anglers such as Kevin find that the pleasures derived from the solitude and scenery of this alpine environment far outweigh the disappointing fishing.

*L*oaded with equipment, Bob Henry inches up a gully on the north side of McGown Peak (right). Digging his crampons into the snow and jamming his ice ax and hammer in ahead of him, Bob led the author and photographer on a five-hour climb. Varied Sawtooth terrain lets climbers clamber up and rappel down precipices, ascend slopes of ice and snow, or hike up sloping boulder fields. Avid fans, Lou Florence and Walt Henderson advertise the sport with their license plate. Here they pack their gear for an ascent. Above, Kevin Swigert scales a rock face to Saddleback Ridge, while Bob Rosso belays from the top, holding the safety rope that would break a fall.

*S*oaking clean after a dusty day, hikers bask in a hot spring near a southern trail head into the Sawtooth Range. Fed by a 20-foot waterfall, this soothing natural spa offers relief and relaxation to bone-weary backpackers. David Kallgren and his wife, Leslie van Barselaar, of Lander, Wyoming, throw off their burdens to enjoy a dip (left), then sprawl contentedly in the mineral water. About a dozen thermal springs bubble in Sawtooth country, but only two lie near the 300 miles of trails that thread the wilderness. The Sawtooths attract more and more visitors each year; the number has tripled in the last decade, reaching 21,000 in 1979.

North Woods

White Birches and Timber Wolves In Mid-America's Verdant Forests

By Dean Rebuffoni
Photographs by Annie Griffiths

The Gunflint Trail is a narrow blacktop road that begins on the rock-strewn shore of Lake Superior, then climbs quickly into the rugged hills of northeastern Minnesota. From the crest of the hills, just above the lakeshore village of Grand Marais, you can gaze eastward across the greatest of the Great Lakes. If the day is fair, you see an infinity of blue sky and blue water.

Then the trail plunges into the deep, dark green of the Superior National Forest, more than three million acres of pine, spruce, aspen, birch, and fir. Farther inland, the trail becomes a shaded corridor flanked on both sides by the million-acre Boundary Waters Canoe Area Wilderness, a watery filigree of more than 1,000 lakes and 1,500 miles of canoe routes.

On the first weekend of summer, my wife, Cathy, and I drove up the Gunflint Trail. We were bound for Little Mayhew Lake, a small, trout-filled body of water that nestles in a quiet corner of the national forest.

We were not alone. Also headed up the Gunflint were camping vans and pickups, cars towing boat trailers, and cars with canoes lashed to their tops. Occasionally a motorcycle, invariably ridden by a young man with a pack and a fishing rod on his back, would flash past. All were headed for the Boundary Waters or for the resorts along the Gunflint.

We parked our car alongside the trail, unloaded our canoe, and carried it down a steep slope to the shore. We paddled across a lake, pulled the canoe out of the water, and carried it across a long, muddy portage to another lake. Then we repeated the process, the "four P's" that are so familiar to canoeists who have plied the interconnected waterways of northeastern Minnesota: put in, paddle, pull out, portage.

The sounds of the traffic on the Gunflint Trail slowly faded behind us. We completed our last portage, and there we were—on the shore of Little Mayhew. For a long while, Cathy and I stood looking quietly across

Chips fly as logger Ron Hartill races to chop through a 14-inch pine log in the 1978 Lumberjack World Championship, held in Hayward, Wisconsin. In 1979, Ron went on to win his sixth straight All-Around Lumberjack title.

43

the lake, 40 acres of placid blue water, deep in the north woods, far from our home in Minneapolis.

"Ah, wilderness," my wife said with a laugh. "It's good to hear that wonderful sound of silence."

We had the lake to ourselves. The trout were uncooperative, but the June day was so warm, so sunny and lazy, that we were content just to paddle slowly around the lake. We went ashore and had lunch on a huge, sun-bleached boulder at the water's edge. Then we wandered through the forest and explored a tiny brook, discovering to our delight that it trickled down from a moss-lined spring hidden in a grove of graceful birches.

We camped that night beside the lake, under a tree canopy, a clear Minnesota sky, and a billion stars. After a long frigid winter and a rainy spring, it was exhilarating to have slipped the bonds of the city to visit a small piece of backcountry in the north woods.

Backcountry. All across this land, all around the great wandering rim of Lake Superior and for miles inland, there are thousands of such places: hidden lakes like Little Mayhew, remote creeks and wild rivers, trails that pass through deep forests, quiet glens, and shaded valleys, across islands, and along rocky shores. There is so much backcountry here, in the north woods of Minnesota, northern Wisconsin, and Michigan's Upper Peninsula, that it is a simple matter to wander down the roads that stretch into the woods, then step off the beaten path, looking for a special place.

I found just such a place one quiet evening in July, while making camp beside Gabimichigami Lake in the Boundary Waters. Our party of eight canoeists had paddled hard all day to reach Gabimichigami, a cold, island-studded lake deep in the wilderness area. Bone-tired from the journey, we sat beside our canoes, beached on the rocks, and listened to the lapping of water on the shore at sunset.

Then we heard the wolves.

Their howling seemed to come from far across the lake, to the north. Then it seemed to come from the east, then the west. There must have been half a dozen wolves out there in the dusk, somewhere in the woods. Their singing was so eerie, so haunting, that not one of us said anything for a long time, until it abruptly ended. "Ah, the children of the night," someone said, quoting from *Dracula.* "What music they make!" We all laughed, but the experience was unforgettable. I have canoed the Boundary Waters many times, but until that evening I had never heard or seen a sign of a wolf there.

Outside of Alaska, the timber wolf exists in the United States in wild, free populations only in Minnesota, although about 40 are protected in Michigan's Isle Royale National Park in Lake Superior. Minnesota has an estimated 1,000 to 1,200 wolves, many of them in the Boundary Waters area or elsewhere in the Superior National Forest.

Because of the unique natural features of the Boundary Waters, the area has long been the object of intense preservation efforts by concerned citizens. It is the largest federal wilderness east of the Rocky Mountains, stretching more than 110 miles along the Minnesota-Ontario border. Though diminished, its virgin forests of spruce and red and white pine are still the largest remaining in the eastern United States.

Protection of the area began early in the century, but since then there has been a continuing battle over how the U. S. Forest Service should manage the Boundary Waters. Preservationists have sought to ban logging, mining, motorboating, and snowmobiling. But loggers and other local interests, including resort owners along the fringe of the area whose

Mid-America's north woods stretch across the upper third of three Great Lakes states and edge the broad expanse of Lake Superior. Minnesota includes the three-

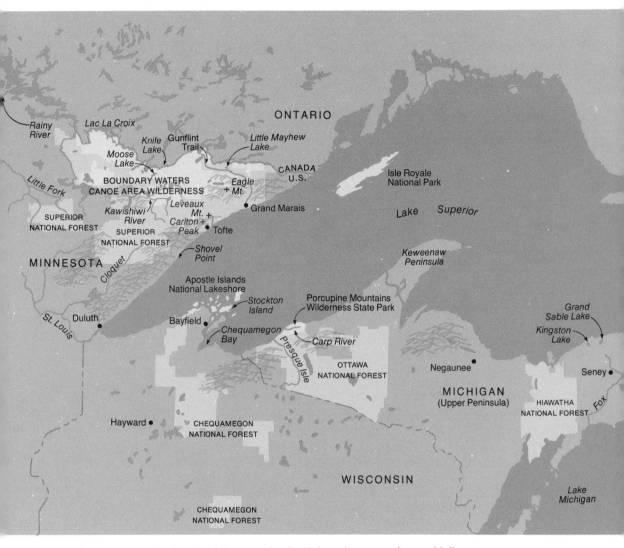

million-acre Superior National Forest, a land of lakes, forests, and rugged hills. The rural Upper Peninsula of Michigan differs greatly from the state's industrial lower half; its citizens have even proposed separate statehood for their area. The Apostle Islands and the Bayfield Peninsula tip the northland of Wisconsin.

livelihoods are dependent upon a healthy tourist trade, have fought against federal restrictions. The battle has been waged in town hall meetings, in federal courtrooms, and in Congress. It has been largely a paper war of legislation, management plans, and lawsuits.

For the preservationists, a major victory came in the autumn of 1978, when Congress formally added a key word—"wilderness"—to the area's name. The lawmakers also added 50,000 acres of adjacent land to the Boundary Waters and banned logging and mining throughout the area. But Congress decided not to ban motorboats and snowmobiles entirely, although it limited such motorized activity to certain lakes and routes.

Despite its vastness, the nation's only designated canoe wilderness is such a popular lure that a few of the more accessible lakes can be crowded during the summer. At the same time, many of northeastern Minnesota's finest rivers—including the Little Fork, Big Fork, Cloquet, St. Louis, and Vermilion—go largely unnoticed and un-canoed.

There's a good reason for that. With more than 15,000 lakes larger than ten acres in their state, Minnesotans are apt to overlook their 25,000 miles of rivers and streams. Indeed, many visitors drive over, or near, some of the finest fishing and canoeing streams in Minnesota while headed north to the Boundary Waters.

Photographer Annie Griffiths and I canoed one of those overlooked streams in July. The Little Fork River rises in Lost Lake Swamp, a flat, marshy area near Vermilion Lake, and flows 150 miles to the northwest into the Rainy River, which forms part of the long boundary between Minnesota and Ontario.

Our trip down the river was arranged by Wayne Sames, an environmentalist and self-proclaimed river rat. He has played a major role in the Minnesota Department of Natural Resources' Wild and Scenic Rivers Program, which is designed to provide permanent protection for several of the state's more scenic and undeveloped streams. Also joining us were Kathy Brandl, who works in the rivers program, and Greg Breining, a writer and avid white-water canoeist.

We launched our canoes beside an old iron bridge, under which the Little Fork gurgled quietly. Greg and I paddled one canoe, while Annie sat amidships. Basswood and aspen trees grew close to the water's edge. "This is really an unusual river," Wayne said, as he and Kathy paddled their canoe alongside us. "There's a stretch of almost 40 miles along the Little Fork where you simply don't see any signs of civilization. No cabins, no farms, no roads. Just wilderness."

We came to our first rapid, a long stretch of white water, and pulled ashore. Greg walked downstream across the boulders that lined the river and studied the scene. "When the Little Fork has enough water, it's one fine river," Greg said. "But it rises and drops quickly, and after a dry spell some of the rapids are too low and rocky to run in a canoe. In any case, it always pays to scout ahead. Otherwise, you might get a little wet."

We stayed dry, and after running several sets of rapids went ashore to explore the banks of the Little Fork. In 1937 this was the scene of Minnesota's last big log drive. For the early Minnesota lumberjacks, the prize trees were the huge white and red pines. Little attention was paid then to white cedar, spruce, jack pine, and balsam fir, all of which were scornfully referred to as "small stuff" by the loggers. But after the pine forests were depleted, the woodsmen turned to that small stuff, particularly the cedars, which were widely used for fence posts, railroad ties, and telephone poles.

During the night, clear skies turned to rain clouds, and the morning found us crouched under a tarpaulin strung from four basswood trees. Wayne, sensing that I was feeling gloomy, tried to cheer things up.

"Look," he said, "there's nothing we can do about the rain. So let's eat. I *guarantee* this drizzle will burn off in a while."

We prepared lunch, using an upside-down canoe as our table. Kathy tossed a rich salad of tomatoes, cucumbers, cheddar cheese, olive oil, and vinegar. Wayne and I fried walleye fillets in beer batter, and Annie concocted a wonderful drink of hot chocolate, instant coffee, and brandy. The feast took some of the dampness out of the day. Then the drizzle stopped— an act of nature for which Wayne willingly took full credit—and we launched our canoes on the quick water to finish our trip. The Little Fork was such a lovely stream that I resolved to visit it again at the end of summer to see what changes autumn might bring.

I've experienced some surprises in the Minnesota woods over the years, but encountering a troll is a surprise indeed. I was hiking up Leveaux

Mountain, had just come over a small rise in the winding trail, and there he was, staring down at me with a wooden grin. I stopped and stared back.

Orton Tofte, who was walking behind me, laughed. "We put Old Troll here to guard the trail," he said. "Some of our young people carved him out of a white cedar log. Looks menacing, doesn't he?"

Orton is an elementary-school teacher who works summers on the North Shore Hiking Trail, which is opening up a big chunk of the Lake Superior backcountry to hikers and backpackers. The trail is part of a system that eventually could wander more than 200 miles through northeastern Minnesota from Duluth to the Canadian border, connecting trails in 13 state parks, three state forests, and the Superior National Forest. Some of the trails, which are being developed by the Forest Service and the Minnesota Department of Natural Resources, are being built by the Youth Conservation Corps, established by Congress to provide teenagers with summer jobs in the outdoors and a basic environmental education.

Orton Tofte is employed by the Forest Service as a YCC supervisor, and during the summer is in charge of 14 teenagers working on the trails. He is 32 years old and lives, appropriately enough, in Tofte, a lakeshore hamlet named after his Norwegian ancestors. He exemplifies the home-is-best thinking of many natives of the north woods.

"I always thought everybody loved where they came from," he said. "I always have. I was raised to believe in my hometown. When I was in college in Minneapolis, I met a lot of students who wanted to get away from their homes. Not me. I'm staying here, close to Lake Superior. I'll always want to be close to Big Blue."

When I visited Orton in July, he was showing his YCC charges how to hew a rough trail out of the thick woods on Leveaux Mountain. Now, in fact, there is not a mountain truly worthy of the word in Minnesota, Wisconsin, or Michigan. The highest point in the three states is Minnesota's 2,301-foot Eagle Mountain, which isn't likely to impress a visitor from, say, Colorado or California.

But Leveaux Mountain, 85 miles up the lakeshore from Duluth, has its charms. I sat at its 1,550-foot summit, looking westward across the national forest, while Orton explained the trail project. "There are so many wonderful, hidden things down there," he said, waving his hand toward the wooded valley of the Onion River, a small stream that flows from the forest into the great lake.

"We should be able to provide a way for people to get into that valley to see what's there: wildlife, ponds and creeks, some nice stands of timber. There's always a surprise waiting for you, and you don't have to be a trained naturalist to enjoy it. Unfortunately, the underbrush is so thick that, unless you're tough or foolhardy, you just don't walk off the road into this country. But the trails we're building will help change that. They complement the natural environment. The deer use these trails, and so do the moose and the bears."

As we talked, some of the YCC workers walked past, carrying hoes and shovels and pushing a wheelbarrow. They wore hard hats and were grimy and sweaty from their work on the trail.

"These kids are amazing," Orton said. "They work six hours a day at this backbreaking work, but they love it. They spend another two hours a day in environmental-awareness courses, and a lot of them are fast becoming amateur naturalists. They learn to spot the little beauties in nature— flowers alongside the trail, bear tracks, deer. You can't experience that sort of thing in the cities."

That evening I hiked with Orton, his wife, Karen, and their two little girls, Solveig and Karina, to the top of another Minnesota "mountain": Carlton Peak, just above Orton's hometown. The path wandered through deep woods of white birch and fir, and everywhere along the way there were raspberry bushes. We would hike awhile, then stop and enjoy some of the ripe, juicy berries.

We reached Carlton Peak, and while waiting for the sunset, sat talking and drinking hot chocolate. Orton, who teaches his schoolchildren about trolls, delighted Solveig and Karina with stories about them. "The Easter Bunny and the Tooth Fairy: They're not real. But trolls! Trolls *are!* There are trolls here in the woods, so watch out!" he told his daughters, who ran shrieking with laughter across the top of the mountain.

At sunset, the view stretched across the great western arm of Lake Superior—Orton Tofte's Big Blue—to the Wisconsin shoreline. We could see, far off to the southeast, veiled in the evening mist, the Apostle Islands and Wisconsin's Bayfield Peninsula.

On a hot August day I drove up the peninsula from Bayfield, a lakeshore town with a picture-postcard resemblance to a New England fishing village. I wanted to visit some of the new breed of young people who are moving out of the cities and into the north-woods backcountry. Walt Pomeroy, a friend who then lived in Bayfield, had urged me to come. "A lot of young folks talk about getting back to the land, about living off the soil, but Tom and Maddy Hart practice what they preach," he said. "Go visit them."

The scene that greeted me as I drove down a narrow dirt road to the Harts' farm was delightful: a small piece of down-home, bucolic northern Wisconsin. There were two goats, a rooster, and two dozen chickens behind the fence beside the barn. An old bathtub and a forgotten rag doll lay in the weeds. There was a big and bountiful garden of tomatoes, cauliflower, parsnips, zucchini, sweet corn, sweet peas, and half a dozen other vegetables. Morning glories clung to the sides of the farmhouse, one of a tumble of old wooden buildings, all surrounded by the deep, dark, Wisconsin woods. I was greeted by the crowing of the rooster.

Thomas Hart was out behind the house, restoring a root cellar that had fallen into disrepair years ago. He greeted me with a smile, apologized for the dirt on his dungarees, and explained that he would use the cellar to store Madeline's canned vegetables and his homemade, fermented specialty: a bottled brew of apple cider and maple syrup.

For $30 a month, the Harts lease five acres of sandy soil near the Raspberry River, just inland from the blunt tip of the Bayfield Peninsula. The 80-year-old farm had been vacant for more than 30 years when they moved in a couple of years ago, and the farmhouse had no electricity, no gas heat, no telephone, no running water. The Harts left things that way.

"We live pretty good lives up here," Thomas said. "We throw ourselves on the elements and hope that the Lord will provide. It sounds simple, but that's just the way we like it: simple."

Thomas, who is 27, looks the part of a backcountry homesteader: tall and lean, with a bushy beard and a red bandanna wrapped around his head to hold back his blond hair. Madeline, at 26, is calm and quiet. They have two little daughters and an infant son.

"Some people probably wonder what it's like for our children, living so far from the cities," Thomas said. "Now, I (Continued on page 65)

Cascading stream rushes around and over rock ledges in a Minnesota pine forest. Such rapids once forced Indians and voyageurs in birchbark canoes to portage; today they halt the numerous canoeists who paddle these waters.

*S*napped paddle in mid-rapid means trouble for Bert Hyde and Andrée Stetson, caught in the foaming current of the Kawishiwi River. At right, they improvise a splint of alder saplings and tape. "Careless," they agree, "not to have brought a spare." The two work for the Outward Bound School in Minnesota. Dorothy Molter (far right) has lived on an island in Knife Lake since the thirties—in a tent in summer and in an old log cabin in winter. She sells homemade root beer—at 25 cents a bottle—to some 6,000 visiting boaters each year.

FOLLOWING PAGES: *Sunset gilds the glassy surface of Lac La Croix in the Boundary Waters Canoe Area Wilderness. Controversy swirls around these placid waters as environmentalists, resort owners, loggers, miners, landowners, and government agencies argue how best to use and preserve the area.*

JIM BRANDENBURG (BELOW)

Cattails and water lilies seem to drift among clouds reflected in a Minnesota lake. Wetlands around such northern waters swarm with life. A bittern (left), stalking frogs or small fish, will freeze into a vertical stance if alarmed, and nearly disappear amid the waving marsh reeds. Fingertip-size, a spring peeper clings to a mushroom. Its shrill cry announces the approach of spring even before the snow has entirely melted. Tiny bees in search of nectar will enter the mauve-striped "toe" of a showy lady's slipper orchid (right). The exits dust them with pollen, which they carry from flower to flower.

Whirling dancers celebrate a wedding at Kawishiwi Lodge in Minnesota's Superior National Forest. Below, Cheryl Larsen dances the Virginia reel with her new husband, Paul Bauman. After taking their nuptial vows in a circle of red pines (right), the bride and groom light a wedding candle (left). The lodge has become increasingly popular with couples looking for a natural setting for a wedding. Both Cheryl and Paul work for the U. S. Forest Service and "spend as much time in the wilderness as we can," says Cheryl. "The outdoors holds a lot of meaning for us. It's a place where we can find direction for our lives, as well as relaxation."

*R*ain-drenched tamaracks fringe a stream in the heart of a conifer swamp-forest in Minnesota. Many such meandering thoroughfares link lakes in the north woods. The bog laurel (left), smaller than its cousin the mountain laurel, glows in a marshy area. Black bears (right) prowl a flower-sprinkled meadow on the outskirts of Tofte, Minnesota. Attracted by refuse, bears have long been a nuisance around north-woods towns.

*P*layful present—a sprig of Juneberry—tempts Bowser, a yearling white-tailed deer. Researcher Mary Shedd offers the morsel. Ordinarily, during this Forest Service study of deer habitat, Mary did not interfere with Bowser's choice of food. Observed from birth, the doe roams free in the Kawishiwi area of Superior National Forest. At lower left, Mary rotates an antenna that tracks beeps from a radio on the deer's collar. Below, Mary and Bowser rest in a shady glade. Researchers here have studied Bowser and other deer around the clock and in every season. Recalling a night spent huddled in a sleeping bag "in below-zero weather," one observer remarked: "We understood then why no one had ever attempted to study deer that way before!" The region's deer population declined 90 percent in the decade ending in 1978. Biologists blame the decrease largely on dense, maturing forests that provide less browse, partly on too much hunting, and partly on unusually severe winters and deep snows that have made predation easier for wolves. Through this and other studies, the Forest Service hopes to learn how to maintain an ecological balance in the wilderness.

*R*aging Lake Superior lashes a rocky shore near Shovel Point, Minnesota. "It is wild, masterful . . . " wrote one Canadian of the vast body of water that dominates the surrounding land, warming it in winter and cooling it in summer. Its clear, clean waters delight fishermen and tourists; wildlife inhabits its forested shores. At far left, a groundhog peers over a lichen-covered rock. A boreal owl nests in a balsam fir along the Gunflint Trail. The boreal usually breeds farther north, but this owl and its mate hatched five owlets here, in the first nesting recorded south of Canada.

want my kids to know what life is like in the cities, and they will. But I want them always to remember the real smell of home, and to know that they can always come back here when city life gets to be too much of a burden. And it will."

The Harts' life is simple but rigorous. In spring they make maple syrup and in summer they garden. Autumn is woodcutting and apple-gathering time. During the long Wisconsin winter they weave handsome wool blankets, rugs, parkas, ponchos, and linen tablecloths that earn them about $4,000 a year. As Thomas said, "We can make it on that, just as long as we keep our costs low."

Scattered in Lake Superior around the tip of the Bayfield Peninsula are the jewels in Wisconsin's crown, the Apostle Islands. Fair weather attracts sailors to this archipelago of sand and rock, and during the summer the blue waters are dotted with white sails. But most of the Apostles remain wild. They have been protected since 1970, when Congress created Apostle Islands National Lakeshore. Although they are believed to have been named by a French Jesuit missionary after Christ's 12 disciples, there are, in fact, 22 of the isles. They range from 3-acre Gull Island to 10,000-acre Stockton Island. Twenty of them have been included in the national lakeshore.

When he was a younger man, Dave Nourse netted herring and whitefish in the frigid waters around the Apostles. But at 72, he doesn't journey out on the big lake much, preferring to stay close to the house he has lived in since he was a year old.

It's a grand old house, wood and stone, built nearly a century ago, and it sits on a hill overlooking Chequamegon Bay, an arm of Lake Superior. Its 13 big rooms are heated by a wood furnace, and Dave cuts the wood.

But there are 80 acres of trees on Dave's 280 acres that he and his wife, Holly, 70, insist will never be cut. Those trees are sugar maples, some more than 100 feet tall and 500 years old. The maples are the Nourses' sugar bush, and each spring Dave and his brother Harvey tap them for their sap, which is boiled down into the pure maple syrup that the Nourses sell.

I walked through the sugar bush with Dave and Holly, admiring the great maples. One huge old tree, its hoary bark the home of clusters of white oyster mushrooms, towered above the others.

"Oh, when this tree comes down it will shake the earth," Holly said. "But it will fall in its own good time, because it will never be cut."

"I used to tap it for sap," Dave said. "But not anymore. I don't want to do anything to hurt this tree. I want to see it outlast me."

As I left the Nourses, Dave said, "I've lived here all my life, and I've never wanted to be anywhere else. This was a wonderful place to grow up, and it still is."

The French explorer and fur-trader, Pierre Esprit Radisson, expressed the same kind of feeling about the Wisconsin country in the late 1660's. "I can assure you I like noe country as I have that wherein we wintered . . ." Radisson wrote. "The country was so pleasant, so beautifull & fruitfull that it grieved me to see that the world could not discover such inticing countrys to live in."

But the world has discovered northern Wisconsin. On any summer weekend, the highways leading to its lakes, rivers, and woods are crowded with cars and campers from Milwaukee, Chicago, and other cities to the

Spray explodes nearly 100 feet into the air as waves crash over a rocky point on Lake Superior, drenching two hikers during a summer storm. "The most refreshing shower I've ever had," one of them said later.

south. Many Minnesotans also journey here on weekends. To me, northern Wisconsin has a softer, tamer, lusher tone than northeastern Minnesota. The two states share in the north woods, but Minnesota's portion seems wilder and more rugged, with a sharper edge to its air.

But for the true character and charm that I associate with the north woods, I think that neither state can match Michigan's Upper Peninsula. The U.P., as its natives call it, may not have the wilderness expanses of Minnesota, but it retains, in its people and its land, an almost frontier atmosphere of independence and solitude. Some residents have proposed— sometimes seriously, sometimes with tongue firmly in cheek—that the peninsula become a separate state, named Superior.

That wouldn't be a bad choice of a name. Lake Superior throws its mighty breakers all along the northern shore of the 300-mile-long peninsula, and one is never far from its waters.

Nor from its woods. Two great national forests, the Ottawa and the Hiawatha, sprawl across the peninsula, and there are vast wooded tracts owned by logging companies. While thousands of acres once covered with white pines have been cut and now support lesser trees, more than 80 percent of the peninsula remains wooded.

The best of these woods are in the Porcupine Mountains Wilderness State Park, near the westernmost tip of the peninsula. Park Ranger Wayne Komsi greeted me as I drove in. "I've never seen so many campers," he said. "I guess civilization is finally catching up with us here."

I had hurried to reach the park, driving across northern Wisconsin ahead of a wall of dark clouds. The storm hit shortly after I made camp, providing me with some excellent entertainment that August night: lightning, claps of thunder, and—after the storm had passed to the east—the wonderfully soft pitter-patter of summer rain.

If civilization is catching up with the Porcupine Mountains—the "Porkies" to backpackers—I wouldn't have known it the next day. I wandered down a trail that passed alongside the Presque Isle River, then entered an expanse of virgin timber. The tallest trees were venerable white pines, and in their shade grew stands of hemlock—lovely, lofty evergreens with conical tops and branches of short, dark, feathery needles. I stood alone in the forest, the only sound the slow drip from the previous night's rain, and watched the sunlight fall through the thick foliage. The light played upon the forest floor in spots and patches of gold, tan, and yellow.

Although miners and lumbermen thoroughly explored the Porkies years ago, they left untouched much of what is now a 58,000-acre park, a majestic mix of streams, lakes, wooded hills, and rocky ridges. Michigan is keeping things wild, banning disposable glass and metal containers from the park, prohibiting mechanical transportation on its foot trails, and protecting its virgin timber. When the trees die and fall, they remain on the land to nourish the soil.

John Walstrom, a native of the Upper Peninsula, sees the woods in a different light.

"I got sawdust in my blood," he said, "and when I see some tall timber, I think about how many logs it will produce at my mill. When I see a tree rotting on the ground, I see wasted logs. Now, I love the woods, I dearly do, but logging is my life."

I visited John at his sawmill, in an area known as Liminga, a lovely piece of backcountry just below the Keweenaw Peninsula and a few miles inland from Lake Superior. This is copper country, and at one time Michigan was our largest producer of the metal, most of which was mined in Keweenaw and elsewhere on the Upper Peninsula. But nearly all of the mines are gone, and in many places the forest is reclaiming the land.

John Walstrom's sawmill sits at the end of a dirt road, in a wide clearing surrounded by forest. John is a big man, 66 years old, with gray hair, a small mustache, a gravelly voice, and an intensely independent outlook on life. He showed me around his mill, past the logs, the big saws, the piles of sawdust, and the stacks of fragrant, cut lumber.

"It smells good here, and every wood smells different," he said. "When you cut oak, it smells like sauerkraut. Maple smells sweet, like something sweet cooking in the kitchen pot."

John's life in the woods began at an early age. His parents had a farm at the edge of the Michigan copper country, but it was on rocky soil. As a boy, John's job was to pick the rocks out of the fields so his father could plow. "But that wasn't my idea of a happy life," he said. "So whenever I could, I'd disappear into the woods. My dad couldn't find me there, and I got to know every tree and creek around these parts. I learned a lot about forestry out there. I was a woods foreman when I was only 24 years old. So, timber cruising just came naturally to me."

They're mostly gone now, but the old timber cruisers were hardy men who were sent into the woods to locate and appraise timber. It was hard, solitary work. A cruiser might spend weeks alone in the wilds, determining how much marketable timber stood on a given tract. John Walstrom cruised timber in Michigan, Ontario, and Minnesota. "Now I got my own little piece of land, 20 acres, and I wish I was a boy again," he said. "So I could watch my trees grow tall and straight."

Natural wonders abound throughout the Upper Peninsula, but I was intent upon visiting one special piece of backcountry: the Fox River, near the old logging town of Seney. This was to be a pilgrimage, a paying of homage to the memory of Ernest Hemingway and to his story, *Big Two-Hearted River*, a classic tale of the outdoors. It is the story of Nick Adams, the young protagonist of many of Hemingway's short stories, and was inspired by the author's real-life adventures in Seney and along the Fox in 1919.

This requires an explanation. There *is* a Two-Hearted River, a fine trout stream that flows through the Upper Peninsula. But the river at Seney, the river that Hemingway fished, is the Fox. He purposely changed its name for the story, explaining later that this was done "not from ignorance nor carelessness but because Big Two-Hearted River is poetry."

On a quiet August evening, Wayne Sames and I camped beside the Fox, which meanders through a woody, marshy region amid flat sand plains. We stayed up late, watching our campfire burn down to bright embers and talking about Hemingway, Nick Adams, and trout fishing.

At dawn, we walked down to the Fox. I had planned to fish the river by wading, as Nick Adams had done, but one look at the Fox changed my mind. The river had been swollen by the summer rains. It ran too fast and deep for wading, and its banks were too bushy to allow fly casting. So we launched our canoe.

But canoes are not meant to be used for fishing, particularly not on quick, narrow, and winding trout streams. Ours kept bumping into the banks. I repeatedly threw my line into the brush and the trees hanging over the water, snarling the leader and forcing us to stop to untangle it. After canoeing about four miles, with not a nibble to show for my angling, we gave up, went ashore, and had lunch.

"So much for Nick Adams and the Big Two-Hearted," said Wayne, announcing that he was returning to camp to take a nap. I was equally disappointed, but I wanted to salvage my pilgrimage, so I walked into Seney.

During the 1880's and 1890's, when the lumberjacks were cutting through the virgin stands of white pine, Seney was the toughest, hell-raisingest spot in the Upper Peninsula. The tales of those days are as tall as the pines, but there's no doubt that Seney was the home of some bigger-than-legend frontier characters.

One was P. K. Small, a local loafer who earned the nickname "Snap Jaw" because he regularly won free drinks at Seney taverns by biting off the heads of live snakes and frogs. One version of the story says that Snap Jaw met his end when he extended his talents and bit off the head of a small owl, the pet of a burly lumberjack. The angry woodsman cracked Snap Jaw's head with the handle of a peavey, a tool used in handling logs.

Things have quieted down in Seney, and today it's a drowsy little town. I inquired at a restaurant if there were any old-timers who might have been around in 1919. The answer was quick in coming: See Jack Riordan. I found Jack at his home, just a short walk from the Fox. He is a retired railroad man, 84 years old, pleasant and talkative, and also the local historian. Best of all, I learned that he was a telegrapher at the Seney depot that summer when young Hemingway stepped off the train, carrying a leather fishing-rod case.

"Yes, I remember him," Jack said. "But my acquaintanceship with Ernest Hemingway was very brief. He got off the train here, and the first thing he did was ask me if I knew where the Fox River was."

I listened intently, scribbling in my notebook.

"So I walked with Hemingway down to the river, down to the old rail-road bridge over there," Jack said. "He could see them big trout down in the water, just finning away. He got all excited. I could hardly keep him from throwing a fly out on the river.

"Anyway, Hemingway took his pack, put it on his back, and went walking north, up an old railroad grade. I never saw him again after that."

It wasn't much, just a chance encounter between two young men long ago, but I was pleased, thinking that I had captured a little piece of forgot-ten history. But something about it bothered me, so I asked Jack if anyone else had inquired about Ernest Hemingway.

"Ha!" he said. "A lot of people come through here asking me about him. Mostly reporters and writers. You must be the twentieth person to ask me about Hemingway. I tell 'em all the same story."

On the last weekend of the summer, on a crisp September Sunday, I returned to Minnesota's Little Fork with two fellow writers. The river had changed. The recent dry days had taken their toll, and the water was low. In the rapids, the clear stretches of water through which we had canoed in July now looked formidable, filled with the jutting tops of boulders that had been covered earlier. But the day was perfect, if a bit cool. I knew that all through the north woods the summer was ending. Quiet streams were drying up, the foliage was turning to its autumn shades, the animals were preparing for another winter.

What I didn't know then, as we slid slowly downstream amid the changing colors of the trees, was that the Little Fork was holding a surprise or two in store for us: a long, exciting run of white water, a mishap, a dunk-ing in the cold, cold water.

But who wouldn't pay so small a price for an autumn trip through "such inticing countrys"?

Wooded hillsides reach the horizon in Michigan's Porcupine Mountains Wilderness State Park. The Carp River flows along a wrinkle in the tapestry of trees.

"*If we forget our past, we can't understand where we're headed,*" *says 75-year-old Frank Matthews. Frank lives in Negaunee on Michigan's Upper Peninsula. Since boyhood, he has collected mining artifacts, and people have presented other relics to him unsolicited. "For a while," he says, "I was afraid to leave home; I'd come back to find things in the yard too heavy to move." In 1969 Frank opened the Jackson Mine Museum in Negaunee to house his collection. Here he lights a miner's candlestick from the mid-1800's. Recreation has now joined forestry and its products and mining as the primary sources of income on the Upper Peninsula. Visitors find sand beaches, such as the one at Grand Sable Lake (below), where an ancient glacial lake retreated. A few miles away stands a decaying stump (opposite, below), remnant of a white-pine forest that fell to loggers long ago. Blueberries ripen at its base.*

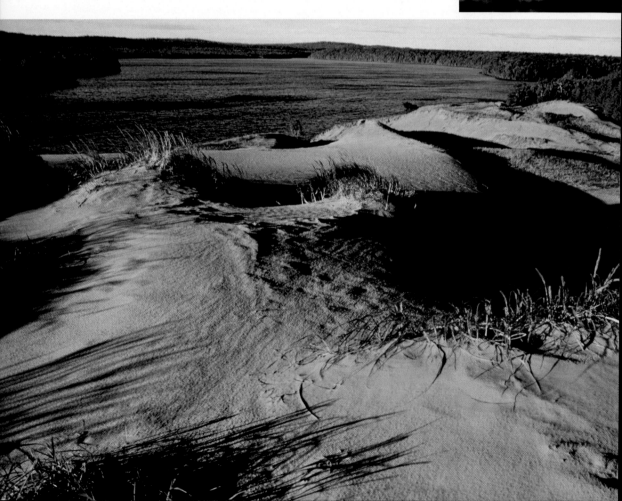

71

*L*acy-leaved ferns carpet a forest floor near Kingston Lake on the Upper Peninsula. Shelf fungi grow on a dead birch tree. Feeding on decaying vegetation, the fungi eventually turn wood into rich humus that feeds new growth. The white birches here replace logged pine trees. In an autumn-tinged stand of birch and aspen trees on Michigan's Isle Royale National Park, an impressive rack crowns a bull moose, and signals the approach of fall. During the winter, the animal will shed it, then begin to grow a new rack the following spring. Wings whirring, a female ruby-throated hummingbird sips nectar from a thistle. By midsummer, the red squirrel must begin gathering cones and seeds for the winter. Summer's short season in the north woods—a few warm months bracketed by severe winters—bursts with such varied life.

"*I* love trees," says Bill Greenwald. "*My name in German means green forest.*" In the house he built near Chequamegon National Forest, the 29-year-old Wisconsin native chats with a neighbor, Desiree DeMars. Bill collected materials for three years before building the three-story structure, salvaging his front door from his great-grandfather's house and using carpet samples for the floor. Below, Desiree and her sister, Lisa, join Bill in preparing a salad of homegrown vegetables. Later, Bill strums an improvised dulcimer, using a cooking pot for a sound box.

Atchafalaya

Cajuns, Crawfish, Cottonmouths: Roaming a Louisiana Swamp

Text and photographs by
Yva Momatiuk and John Eastcott

We headed south in the thickening heat of August, my husband John and I, and Miś, our part-Samoyed dog. In southern Louisiana the air grew moist and sweet, and the land flattened out beneath cotton plants, soybeans, sugarcane, and live oaks. Near Baton Rouge, Old Man River nudged us with a massive elbow, and the steamy breath of the Gulf of Mexico stirred the waters of little bayous bordering the highway.

"Miś, you'd better start watching for alligators," said John, who was driving. "They seldom bother people, but . . ." he paused dramatically, "they gulp down dogs. Especially large white dogs."

Actually we had no idea who would eat whom during our three months in the Atchafalaya, the country's largest floodplain swamp. Its wild and wet body stretches for 75 miles through 700,000 acres of bayous, lakes, willow stands, and cypress-tupelo forests near the instep of Louisiana's boot. It comprises roughly half of the entire Atchafalaya Basin, whose head is a water-control structure near Simmesport, and whose toes soak in the marshland of the Atchafalaya delta below Morgan City.

While the Mississippi River drains nearly half the contiguous United States, near its lower end the Atchafalaya River, its main distributary, conveys about a fourth of its flow and the worst of its spring floodwaters on a shortcut to the Gulf. Waters of the Red River also join the Atchafalaya near Simmesport. For the fishermen, trappers, and hunters who settled around "chaff-uh-LIE-uh," the swamp is a giant aquatic calendar, measuring seasons and life cycles. It is the pulse of Cajun country, where some of the Acadians expelled by the British from Nova Scotia found refuge during the early 19th century. Here they learned from the Chitimacha and Houma Indians how to live off the land. Swamp names—Atchafalaya, Hooppole Bayou, Bayou L'Embarras, Crook Chene, Bayou Ramos, Pat's

Sunrise burnishes shallow Lost Lake in the Atchafalaya swamp. Cypress stumps and young trees break its mirror surface. The name—locally pronounced "chaff-uh-LIE-uh"—derives from a Choctaw Indian phrase meaning "long river."

Throat, Four Hundred Dollar Bayou, Buffalo Cove—are the legacy of early Indian, Spanish, French, and English settlers.

But how do you explore a watery kingdom that seems to poke fun at the U. S. Geological Survey charts, which are unable to keep pace with the ever-changing swamp? Having been nomadic for many years, John and I had learned how to find our way around in the backcountry: If maps offer little help, look for people who love the place. I called a local number: "Is this the Sierra Club?"

"It sure is, ma'am." A soft, feminine drawl eased me down among satiny pillows. "What can we do for you, honey?"

"Could I speak to anyone who knows the Atchafalaya swamp?"

"Honey, I have this awful feelin' you've got the wrong place. This is a lounge. You come here to enjoy yourself, do a little drinkin', do a little laughin'. . . ." Later we located a chapter of the environmentalist Sierra Club in Baton Rouge, and joined two of its members for our first look at the Atchafalaya.

The Bayou Sorrel landing looked like a crowded drive-in movie theater, except that every vehicle had a boat trailer attached. Their owners had gone into the swamp. "At dawn people line up for miles to reach the ramp," said Charles Fryling, Jr., who teaches landscape architecture in Baton Rouge. He lowered his canoe into the current. "But their motorboats are only good for fishing along the main channels. The most beautiful parts of the swamp are hard to reach during low water. You have to paddle, portage, and walk."

"Do you ever use waders?" I asked him.

"Only in the winter; tennis shoes are so much lighter."

I like animals—including the creeping, crawling, and other less popular varieties. But a vivid image of cottonmouths wrapped around my knees, of leeches feasting on my ankles, and of alligators taking care of the rest was a trifle unsettling. What about them? Charles and his wife, Doris Falkenheiner, a Baton Rouge lawyer, laughed: "Hah! Don't forget nests of wasps and fire ants." Off we went, doubts unresolved.

The day was humid and hot. We followed a canal that was part of an extensive network dug for oil and gas pipelines. The water was shallow, yellow-brown, the forest seemingly lifeless under the blazing sun. But Miś stood erect in the bow, mesmerized by a symphony of smells. They meant animals . . . many animals.

The canal ended in mud. Soft rain began to fall. We carried our canoes over a beaver dam and into a deep, dark pond. The green forest closed behind us, and our footprints filled with black ink. I suddenly felt like a child who has crawled under a leafy canopy and covered all betraying tracks: If I keep still and breathe quietly, no one will find me.

I love mud. I love its sticky, solid substance, its mysterious depth, the way it sucks at my toes with soft, smacking gurgles or deep, rumbling grunts. Atchafalaya mud is a dream goo, smelling cleanly of decaying plants. Oily black when wet, it dried gray and silky on my skin.

The cypress trees stood in the pond like organ pipes. Ferns shone green. Viceroy butterflies made unhurried love among the nebulous flowers of the buttonbush. We paddled slowly, quietly. Suddenly—birds! Five great egrets took off, moving their huge white wings in elaborate sweeps, necks erect, feet dangling. They picked up speed, slalomed gracefully among the trunks, and disappeared. Their determined departure was superbly theatrical, as if nothing in the world could hold them back.

"Look!" said Charles. High in a cypress tree there was another bird, an anhinga, crucified. Its twitching black wings were spread wide like a broken umbrella, embracing air that no longer meant freedom. A thread ran out of its throat and up, snagged in the branches. We reached the trunk, and Charles climbed it gingerly until a branch sounded a warning and he could go no farther. A pocket knife . . . stretch . . . cut. The bird hit the water and sank. Charles descended quickly, pulled it out, extracted the fishhook that was imbedded in its throat, and let it rest and dry in his canoe. Anhingas are accomplished fishers, but after diving usually have to dry their waterlogged wings. How did this one manage to entangle itself? "Water birds raid the trotlines that fishermen tie low between the trees. They swallow the fish—hook and all—and fly away, tangling the line in the branches." Our bird revived and swam off among the young trees.

"These trees won't be here next year," said Doris. "Too much water. A young cypress needs about four years before it takes full root. The U. S. Army Corps of Engineers' flood-control program has altered the watering and dewatering cycle, so I doubt that we will see another great cypress forest here if we cut or destroy the existing trees."

River waters spread at will in the lower Atchafalaya Basin until 1927, when 800,000 people along the Mississippi suffered the worst flood in memory. After this disaster the corps designated the basin a floodway system for the Mississippi, and extended levees to channel floodwaters to the Gulf. Other corps control measures have thus far successfully prevented the Atchafalaya from capturing the Mississippi entirely, an eventuality that would one day leave Baton Rouge and New Orleans as backwaters.

Our canoes floated side by side. A gentle rain fell and we soaked in it, cooling off, watching mullet jump and counting their powerful leaps. Alligator gars, toothy and fast, pursued their prey into the green jungle. Water snakes came out, draping their sleek, supple bodies on low branches.

High-water marks on the trees were six feet above our heads. The Atchafalaya-Mississippi river system brings nutrients from the fertile soils of mid-America. After the high water recedes, these nutrients help support plants that feed an animal community that Dr. Fred Bryan of the U. S. Fish and Wildlife Service believes is at least as abundant and certainly more diverse than that of the Everglades. But the natural life cycle is being shortened by land clearing, irrigation, and flood control along the Mississippi and its tributaries, activities that release such vast quantities of silt that sizable lakes here have diminished greatly in recent decades.

We turned back in the darkening tunnel of green. Charles's paddle flashed in front. In our muscles we felt the first twinges of pain, which only days of paddling would ease. The air cooled. A barred owl flew so low its wings stirred a warm current, like a luxuriant, feathery fan. The night filled with cries and whispers.

"Hey, John," I called softly to my partner of many such green days. "We're going to love it here." I felt joy jumping in me like a silver mullet.

John and I began traveling alone, kept on our toes by the trackless wilderness. We were warned that the swamp folk would be an aloof lot, suspicious toward strangers who do not speak their language, a wonderful old Cajun French that is sprinkled with Indian, Spanish, and English words. One well-wisher advised, "If you try to do any serious fishing in their territory you'll get hazed. Perhaps they won't harm you, but remember, they scrounge their living the hard way, and resent intruders."

We did not dream of fishing. Our ten-foot aluminum bateau, as the flat-bottomed, blunt-nosed swamp boats are called, carried only camping gear, food, cameras, and telescopic lenses. Our encounters with the locals were often similar. "Did you catch all the fish?" they would ask, shifting their outboard engines into neutral to facilitate conversation. Dark, Gallic eyes would stare from under sun visors. Surprised to learn that fishing was not on our minds, they would ask: "Where y'all from? Baton Rouge?" We began to feel that John's New Zealand and my native Poland were just around the corner, and Baton Rouge was the end of the world.

One day we met a fisherman, Buck Lewis, working his nets from a homemade boat. His eyes were a sad blue, his face wrinkled. Buck didn't mind our company.

Hoop nets are ideal for a fisherman working alone. They are made of nylon fiber stretched on fiberglass rings and are baited with cheese, the stinkier the better. Although their location is never marked, they are easy to steal. Buck couldn't find two of his sets and was bitter. "If I catch somebody foolin' with my nets, I ain't gonna need no sheriff. I'm just gonna put him in that water there." He sat down heavily, suddenly old and discouraged. He opened a container of coffee, as black and thick as the Atchafalaya mud. We drank, rocking in our boats and wishing for a better world.

"It's my livelihood. It's like someone takin' your job away. I've got eleven kids." A 25-pound catfish, taken from the last net, flopped near his foot. Buck smiled and hoisted it high. "Talk about beautiful! Me, this's what I eat: *goujon*, yellow cat. Them blue cats are pretty fish but dirty. They eat anything." The swamp teems with catfish, buffalofish, alligator gar, bass, bluegill, crappie, freshwater drum, and above all, crawfish—tiny cousins of the lobster. They are also known as crayfish, crawdads, and mud bugs, and without them the local cooking would not be the same.

We drifted past an old stump, a remnant of the huge cypress forest that was logged here from before the Civil War until the 1930's. The swampers who wrestled with those giants under the blazing sun are gone, too, as if they had died with the trees.

"What's going to happen to the swamp?" asked John.

Buck looked up. "I'm 60 now, and every year I see less water and more sand. I think the landowners are gonna drain it all and build houses on it. Say *you* had a lot of land and could dry it up and sell it, it might just cross your mind to do that."

His fear is justified. Many areas in the northern part of the basin have already been cleared for farming.

September arrived. Blue asters covered muddy ridges; receding water revealed numerous crawfish chimneys rising above the breeding homes the crustaceans make. Our attitude toward wildlife—live and let live—paid off. Wasp nests could be avoided; alligators kept their distance; fire ant stings were bearable. And we developed a "snake sense," for sometimes even when we didn't see or hear anything we would turn slowly and . . . yes, another cottonmouth, unmistakable, stared back from its resting spot. Marvelous, gutsy snakes, cottonmouths—also called water moccasins—often stood their ground as few rattlesnakes would. They emit a scent from musk glands on their tails, but only Miś could smell it.

Harmless water snakes displayed intricate patterns and remarkable fishing skills. We let small ones wander around our fingers; held gently, they seemed to enjoy our warmth and never bit. Big-eyed owls watched these antics disapprovingly: One shouldn't play with one's food.

The seemingly logical way to explore the basin would be to follow the course of the Atchafalaya River, but it is not so. Cargo barges and crew boats travel up and down the main channels, making the treacherous currents even more dangerous for small craft. Powerful dredges maintain navigation channels. Wildlife retreats deep into the swamp.

When we first met Johnny Johnson in Bayou Pigeon, he said: "I could stay in the basin 24 hours a day, 366 days (*Continued on page 97*)

Wary and alert, a mink eyes intruders in the Atchafalaya. Other creatures—
otters, alligators, water birds, muskrats, black bears—share the swamp habitat.

Green waters of Bayou Long lap at the trunks of water-marked cypress trees. The Atchafalaya still rises and falls to the rhythm of spring floods, but within the levees sedimentation confines more and more of the water to channels. This may doom young cypresses, such as the one at far left. It will die if rising levels of silt or water submerge it for too long. At left, writer-photographer Yva Momatiuk and her dog, Miś, glide quietly through the swamp. A nutria (right) gnashes orange incisors when disturbed.

*U*ncertain friendship gets off to a shaky start as Telly Singleton, 4, confronts a slider turtle held by his father, William. The Singletons live on Avoca Island, where they fish and hunt for their livelihood. Although largely dependent on motorboats, they still find the maneuverable pirogues indispensable. At bottom, Telly's brother Calvin poles a pirogue near the docking sheds that shelter their boats. Calvin and his bearded brother, Edward (below), perform a seemingly endless swamp task: repairing outboards.

"*T*he swamp is like a mother; she never fails her children,*" a commercial fisherman told the authors. Buck Lewis (right) has fished the swamp waters for nearly 20 years. Here he empties catfish, buffalofish, and freshwater drum from his hoop nets. High water in 1973 flooded Buck's home near Bayou Sorrel, but—paradoxically—he worries more about the swamp drying up: Thousands of acres both inside and outside the floodways have been cleared and developed. Another fisherman, Antoine Bourque of Catahoula, makes a hoop net as his 5-year-old grandson, Kelly, plays inside.

PRECEDING PAGES: Molten sun dips below the far shore of Grand Lake, once so wide that swamp dwellers could not see across it. In recent decades, continual sedimentation has built long, thin islands, shredding much of the open water into narrow ribbons.

*F*rom nature's larder comes food for a crab boil—a traditional Cajun feast. Rudy Gautreaux, 16, of Baton Rouge, carries the day's catch of crabs to his family's houseboat, moored on Bayou Boutte. In a large pot, ingredients—lemons, potatoes, onions, garlic, bay leaves, peppers, cloves— will boil briskly. The crabs, rinsed and combined with the mixture, will boil until red and succulent. Armed with a knife, Rudy digs in (below). Rudy's family descends from French-speaking Acadians expelled from Nova Scotia by the British in 1755. The Acadians settled in the Atchafalaya early in the 1800's, and today their descendants live in little towns around the swamp and throughout southern Louisiana. Like many other Louisianans, Rudy and his family spend every free weekend at their swamp retreat. A hole in the floor of their houseboat allows them to continue fishing at night or during bad weather. The blue crab, one of the most abundant crustaceans found in Louisiana's coastal waters, supports a sizable crabbing industry.

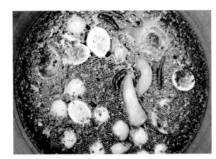

Gnarled cypress knees emerge from a tangle of flowering water hyacinths. Some botanists now believe the knees help supply oxygen to trees with submerged roots. The hyacinth has choked waterways throughout the basin since its introduction, but the dense blanket of plants also provides a hiding place for swamp creatures. A sleek bullfrog (left) finds refuge among its green leaves and lavender flowers. A bug-eyed crawfish (right) waves armored pincers from a leafy perch.

*T*hick morning fog hangs over graves and live oak trees in the Pierre Part cemetery. Every autumn, Pierre Part's Cajun residents scrub and whitewash the tombs and crosses. On October 31—the eve of All Saints' Day—families arrive with armfuls of fresh flowers, and light candles that burn all night and into the next day. The Cajuns of the Atchafalaya maintain strong family ties, and their cemeteries often lie in the center of their towns and villages. One woman said, "I prefer to be buried here in the village. Not that I'll know, I guess, but I feel better, knowing I'll be near my home."

Majestic great egret, dazzling in its whiteness, surveys its watery realm. Two dozen species of water birds—egrets, ibises, ducks, herons, anhingas—nest in the Atchafalaya. They prey on fish, frogs, crawfish, and snakes in the swamp and marshes.

a year, if only I could get that extra day." The next morning before dawn we left together, following Little Bayou Pigeon. The word "bayou" comes from the Choctaw Indian *bayuk,* meaning creek; it now describes almost any kind of Louisiana waterway. Bayous are seldom still. Currents rock their waters, as if to soft lullabies.

The sun rose and sandwiched us between the blue and the green. Johnny's custom-built aluminum fishing boat dove into the swamp, over fallen logs, under hanging branches, up and around cypress knees, through mud, and across lakes. Occasionally Johnny would stalk a bird—just to see how close he could get—paddling with a broad sugarcane knife. Only his brown wrist moved, making small circles. It seemed his dark, shining eyes would hold a bird against dark ranks of trees until we could see every perfect feather, and watch it get up on its toes like a ballerina.

Johnny came to live near the swamp as a wild teenager, and the Atchafalaya "kept him from trouble," his sister believes. Maybe it is this love of the wilderness, maybe his drop of Indian blood, but at 28 he looks as if he had stepped from an old painting full of giant cypresses and lurking alligators. He is very tall, cat-quick, and married to brown-eyed Carolyn. He works as a painter for construction companies during low-water season, but crawfishing and hunting rule his life. Johnny warns Carolyn: "If we ever have a little girl, she'll have a pair of hip boots and a shotgun."

We passed many camps, as Louisianans call their weekend fishing-hunting cabins. Some stood on posts to clear the floods, others floated on pontoons made of oil drums or logs.

In the late afternoon we watched water birds stalking fish on Grand Lake. Ibises worked the shallows, impatiently poking curved beaks here and there, while elegant snowy egrets would march slowly, then freeze strategically and strike.

The setting sun spilled an orange hue among solitary cypress trees standing in the lake. John climbed one to wait for the light of the full moon that was due that night, and Johnny and I drifted toward a roost where thousands of birds come for the night's rest. That night John wrote: "I balanced myself on a limb, aware of the water 40 feet below. As the dusk deepened, the moon rose and I leaned against the sweet-smelling trunk, watching the silhouettes of birds coming to roost. Suddenly, large shapes obscured the moon and, with an abrupt beat of wind, landed just above me, long-toed legs pushed forward, necks curved back, tails dropped. Cypress leaves fell on me like confetti. Three enormous wood storks examined their habitation, unaware of my breathless presence. One scratched its neck, its toes and claws wriggling with purpose. Another caught sight of my tripod and craned its neck for a better look. His enormous beak was so close I could have touched it. Puzzlement, curiosity, and tension were in his face, but he boldly attacked the tripod. His instant recoil had his two companions in flight, and he followed, leaving me suddenly alone."

We headed back. Near an oil platform, several workers were having a midnight swim, their bodies glistening in the moonlight, quiet voices carrying in the warm air.

The low water in the backswamp had forced the animals to work the bayous, and Johnny's spotlight revealed a Tiffany display of shining eyes. Emeralds belonged to raccoons; opossums and muskrats wore opals; nutrias sported golden beads, and bullfrogs displayed white triangular throats like elegant cravats. Deer eyes flashed and were gone. Owls stared from their perches, and other night birds called, hooted, and whistled. A shaggy night heron feasted on a crawfish. A mink ran up on shore, dragging a gleaming fish. He would run a few feet, lie on the fish, wait, drag it a little farther, and lie on it again.

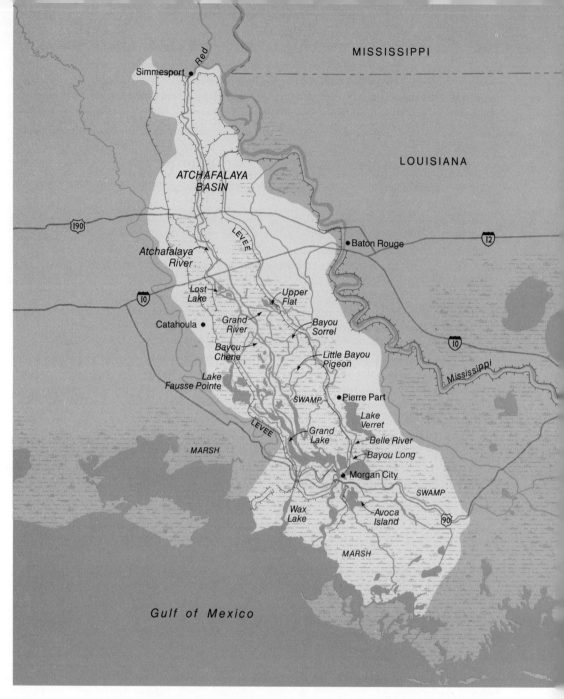

Largest floodplain swamp in the country, the Atchafalaya covers 700,000 acres in southern Louisiana. Levees enclose floodways—large areas of swamp cut by channels—that carry Mississippi River overflow to the Gulf of Mexico. The Atchafalaya Basin lies between present and former courses of the Mississippi.

"He's trying to hide himself without letting go of the fish," whispered Johnny. "We might be another animal, ready to steal his food. He knows the shining fish betrays him."

He spoke dreamily: "I'll tell you honestly, if I had a choice between going to heaven after I die, or back into the swamp, to the days before the logging started . . . I'd take the swamp." Such love deserves an extra day in a year. Perhaps even more.

We left Bayou Pigeon for Morgan City, famous for its annual Shrimp and Petroleum Festival, although nowadays petroleum rules the town.

Manufacturers of drilling equipment crowd the waterfront; large barges thread the Intracoastal Waterway. Extensive levees surround Morgan City like a medieval fortress. Some 30,000 people are threatened here during every big flood. Mayor Russell "Doc" Brownell is furious:

"We live in constant danger. First, the waters from the Rockies to the Appalachians descend in the spring. Then, in late summer, hurricanes bring giant, surging waves and we have the Gulf on top of us. Another flood like the one in 1973 will finish us, unless the Corps of Engineers enlarges the river channel. But since the environmentalists got involved, all the corps can do is studies!" There is a fear, however, that deepening the river might lower the water level of the entire swamp, threatening the whole ecosystem of the Atchafalaya.

South of the busy Intracoastal Waterway we entered the marshland of the delta. Here the sky was endless, and low wetland vegetation predominated: tall grasses, leafy elephant's ears, and water hyacinths, also called lilies, the curse of the waterways. Exactly how the plant came to be introduced into the U. S. is still unclear, but the explanation perhaps stems from the 1884 World's Industrial and Cotton Centennial Exposition in New Orleans. There the Japanese treated each visitor to a pretty flowering hyacinth. Birds carried the seeds into quiet bayous, where the plant flourished. Thick carpets of flowers and leaves, propelled by wind and tide, can choke a waterway in just a few days. The corps and state agencies have fought a never-ending battle throughout the swamp, using a variety of weapons. Pitchforks and a special plant-chewing stern wheel spread the growth; dynamite destroyed everything but the hyacinth; flamethrowers stimulated the plants beautifully. A modern chemical—2,4-D—has brought the hyacinths partly under control.

Near Wax Lake we met a shy fisherman and trapper and his mother, who live in the marsh much the way folks did half a century ago. Their camp boat was compact and spotless. It was surrounded by smaller boats, like a suburban home with half a dozen cars parked before it. Tons of firewood stacked on a large raft would be used to dry animal pelts during the winter.

"I think building that Intracoastal slowed the current in the bayous, which used to keep the lilies cleaned out," said the trapper, his face intense. "But lilies also feed and shelter animals, and keep the sport fishermen away. They get paychecks every week; yet I've seen them come here and stun fish illegally with electric shockers and sell them for profit. This cuts the commercial fisherman's throat. If you worked for a company as hard as we work, you'd be its president in three years!" He looked across the bayou. His face softened. "You know, this land will take care of you, but you must treat it right. Take what you really need, step aside, and leave it alone so it can come back. People don't know when to stop."

Inside I found his mother preparing black Cajun coffee. At 71, with her white hair and serene face, she looked like a granny enjoying the autumn of her life. But her bed was strewn with heavy fishing rods and shotguns. Years ago, when her husband died, she supported her family by fishing and by hunting alligators, getting $1.75 a foot for a seven-foot reptile. She still fishes with nets, rods, and trotlines, proudly remembering her largest catfish, a 65-pound monster.

Later we found that many authorities in the Atchafalaya would disagree with the trapper: Most illegal fishing, they say, is done by commercial fishermen themselves, not by sport fishermen.

Green and lush Avoca Island is south of Morgan City, near the marshlands. There we met Calvin Singleton, a black fisherman who had seen several alligators that morning. We followed him through hyacinths and past wild hibiscus, cattails, and alligator weeds. But the reptiles had apparently retired to their muddy dens. Suddenly, Miś shot off the boat, swam toward the shore, and disappeared. "Alligators gulp down dogs. . . ." rang in my head, but Calvin was faster than my fear, jumping, wading, running, a heavy paddle clenched in his fist. A moment later the green jungle parted, revealing Miś, and Calvin carrying a dead nutria.

"Miś just went crazy! Dogs hate them rats. They have to get them, even if they die doing it." He petted Miś. "Good dog. Them nutrias are mean. Leave Miś with me, we'll hunt together," he joked.

I praised Calvin's willingness to help us. That pleased him: "I want to be such a good Christian that when my time comes people will say, 'Let's see a *good* man die.' " We went to meet his folks, who live on the edge of the Intracoastal Waterway. There were wooden cabins, a church, and an orange grove, heavy with satsuma oranges. Small docks and sheds provided a floating base for bateaux, skiffs, and pirogues, featherlight swamp boats so tippy that it's said "you must part your hair in the middle and never shift your chewing tobacco." John asked Calvin's uncle how long his people had lived on the island.

"Oh Lordy. When Abraham signed his civil rights bill, they were already on Avoca. Good place it was, full of Spanish moss. We sold it to stuff mattresses and pillows and furniture. When people learned you was from Louisiana they'd say: 'Ah, that's where money grows on trees.' It did."

How did the blacks get along with Cajuns, we asked. "In the bayous we don't see colors at all," answered Calvin. "But one day when I went to get me a hamburger in town, the man told me to go to the back door or he'd get the sheriff. I did, but lost my appetite, threw the food on the ground, and cried. That was 15 years ago." Later we ate fried frog legs, and learned that in addition to fish, shrimp, crab, turtles, and ducks, the Atchafalaya larder delivers wild honey, venison, rabbits, squirrels, berries, and herbs. Calvin and his relatives consider themselves Creole. But who are the Cajuns?

"The Cajun is the happiest darn fellow you've ever seen." So we were told in Catahoula during a church fair, a part of the yearly blessing of the sugarcane crop. One of Catahoula's faith healers sat near us during the open-air Catholic Mass. He treated sunstrokes, teething pains, sprains, snakebites—earning nothing but respect as one of the last true *traiteurs,* whose powers, the people believe, come from God. Food was served from vats—jambalaya, gumbo, fried chicken. Beer flowed, men besieged portable blackjack tables, women played *la bourre,* a Cajun mix of bridge and poker. Profits from fairs, which can reach $25,000 during a good crawfish season, go to the church, to a family in need, to the sick.

Many Cajuns live high, spending money as quickly as they earn it. Festivals celebrate crawfish, shrimp, cotton, sugarcane, and racing frogs. During a pig festival, local girls compete for the title of Miss Swine. A Cajun *fais-do-do,* as their dances are called, is a furiously happy affair. The children dance, old men twirl *jolies blondes,* and grannies waltz with teenage boys until the last drop of sweat is spent, and the first roosters crow in the village. *Laissez le bon temps rouler:* Let the good times roll.

Life in Catahoula centers on the family, the ancient unit. Lorena Bourque lives with her bachelor son, Mike. His six married sisters visit daily, bringing their children, a quilt one can finish best under mama's oak tree, a problem to solve, a joy to share. The Bourques talked with us readily in English, but French is their tongue. We savored a variety of smells, spices, and great Cajun cooking. Food is so important that when I asked for a gumbo recipe I received as many as there were Bourque women. They all began: "First, you make your *roux. . . .*"

Gumbo is an African word for okra; roux is French, and means a flour and fat mixture, browned slowly in a heavy pot. The quilter, Dot, explained: "As you pour your flour you have to keep stirring. I like my roux real dark. Then you put in your chopped onions, your celery, bell pepper, and lots of seasoning, and stir it until your onions are clear. Now add your water, and if it's a shrimp gumbo you add shrimp. You can use okra, chicken, sausage, crawfish, anything. If you have more people coming, just add more water." Simple and delicious, it is served over steaming rice. Many Cajun men excel in the art of cooking, discussing gourmet tips as easily as they talk crab traps, catfish boxes, and crawfish bait.

Autumn came crowned with morning fog. Cypress leaves turned rusty, and ducks began arriving for the winter. We headed for Upper Flat, a lake that spreads its cool arms north of Grand River. Water patrolman Jasper Hebert, of the Louisiana State Police, promised to keep an eye on our camper while we were gone. We loaded the bateau until its freeboard amounted to a scant four inches.

A small bateau draws little more water than a canoe and accommodates far more gear, but soon our craft sat abruptly in mud. Like Volga boatmen, we uncoiled a line and pulled the bateau through the mud to the lake. It was a joy to rock on its calm body, and watch thunderheads build up, swirl like white rapids, and disappear. After a wet summer, autumn in the Atchafalaya is usually dry, and for six weeks we didn't have any rain. Many water birds departed for their wintering grounds and were replaced by new arrivals from the north. Fat brown nutrias carried late sun reflected in their whiskers. Raccoons raced along the waterline, searching for morsels with their narrow hands, and playing raccoon games in tall, golden grass. A large mullet jumped into our bateau.

We camped on a boggy island, dined on a gift of roasted teal, the mullet, and shelled pecans. The night was cold, with dew beading on the tent and screech owls holding a meeting overhead. Morning was plastered with thick, gray fog. We had a miserable, wet breakfast, jumping around for warmth. Determined to explore, we set out early.

The fog muffled our tiny outboard. Headless ghosts of giant cypress stumps loomed above. Black vultures feasted on the carcass of a buffalofish, and we crept up for a good look at their alert, cruel eyes, crooked beaks, and white-lined wings. The fog parted. The birds opened their damp wings to the sun, like a coven of witches drying their black robes.

We discovered we could avoid the deepest pockets of mud and walk freely nearly everywhere. Distant rifle shots reminded me of a Cajun who once shot a buck from his pickup's cab, shattering the windshield and battering his eardrums. "I can get myself 50 windshields, but I can't always get a ten-point buck," he explained.

The November nights were cool and starry, the mornings white with fog, but the days still warm. The solitude was so complete we could abandon our clothes and walk and swim in blissful freedom. Once a fat, pregnant nutria charged John, aiming her orange, two-inch teeth at his leg. Only his tripod, used in defense, prevented bloodshed.

Finally we returned and told Jasper about the lake, the ducks and geese, the mammals and fish. "Once there was quite a town up there on Upper Flat, camp boats moored everywhere," he said. "Every week a boat with groceries and mail would come to trade for fish, pelts, and moss. The floodways finished it all. It breaks your heart to see some of the changes."

His eagerness to be helpful amazed us, but Jasper smiled sadly: "I'll do anything for you, or anyone, who might help save the basin."

We had heard it before. People who love and need the swamp consider it a national treasure. But the question of how best to manage it is being argued by several powerful special-interest groups: the landowners, government agencies, environmentalists, and politicians. Many people also believe that the present flood-control system, although deadly for the swamp, is essential for protection against flood damage, and yet is no longer adequate because of siltation. Under mounting pressure, the corps is considering new solutions, including multipurpose plans for land and water use aimed at maintaining the Atchafalaya as a productive wetland and a floodway only. Public hearings are held, tempers fly, bureaucracy turns its unhurried wheels, and the swamp must wait.

Its fate worries newcomers as well as longtime residents. In 1965 Linda Cooke and her husband, Pete, university graduates from Michigan, bought a 20-foot motorboat, packed up baby Becca, and set off down the Mississippi with dreams of reaching South America. Near Baton Rouge, the towering wakes of large tankers deterred them. The Cookes learned of a safer way to the Gulf, through the Atchafalaya swamp. "We had no idea there was a place down south where you could live off the land, as in Canada," reflected Linda. Hers is a face Vikings used to die for: slender, with calm blue eyes, framed by streaming blonde hair.

They decided to stay. That first year they lived in a tent, harassed by hurricane Betsy, the cold muddy winter, and their own lack of experience. They acquired a camp boat; the second daughter, June, was born. Living off the land demanded hard, dirty work, but they loved the freedom and the basic sense of touching the earth. The swamp grew on them.

They took us coon hunting one night. Linda held the dogs, and we plowed north on the black current of Belle River until Pete's spotlight picked out a pair of emeralds. He raced the motor, pushing the bateau onto the bank. The dogs and Linda ran. The raccoon climbed a tree, and Pete brought it down with a single shot. We followed the river until the cold penetrated our bones. It started drizzling, but our luck returned after midnight, and we bagged another. We hurried home, back to the yellow lights of the cypress camp boat, the wood-burning stove, a dinner of raccoon meat, Pete's guitar, and a game of chess. The skins meant a pair of new shoes for June, but when Linda picked up the smaller of the two coons I heard her softly say: "Why did you climb a tree without any branches? You didn't have a chance, poor thing. . . ." The family's pet coon, Coonie-Moonie, looked on wistfully from the kitchen counter, safe and snug.

On our last morning we went to Hooppole Lake, beached our bateau, and walked. John strolled off with Miś to look for edible oyster mushrooms that grow on willows. I turned west along the narrow lake. One side already basked in golden light, catching snowy egrets full blast, while my shore was still dark and somber. Suddenly my instinctive swamp alarm went off: Watch out! Watch out! I looked down.

He was black as midnight, tapering toward a small head. His body was thick, well nourished, ready for winter. The alert eyes, with the vertical pupils of pit vipers, watched me intently—and he was very, very close.

One step back and my heart slowed down. Heavenly white birds chased fish in blue shallows as if nothing had happened. John and Miś were somewhere in the forest. My cottonmouth relaxed without moving a muscle. There was room for us all—Atchafalaya for all of us.

"Like living in a cathedral," says Linda Cooke of the Atchafalaya. Here she paddles homeward with her daughter June. In 1965, the Cookes paused in the swamp on their way to make a new home in South America—and have lived here ever since.

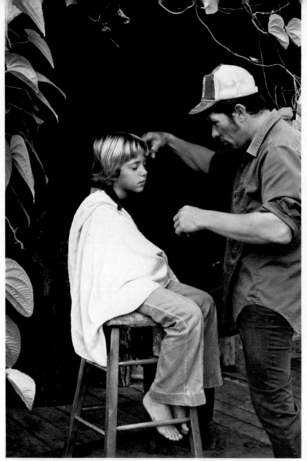

Piggyback ride among cypress knees and stumps keeps June Cooke high and dry; her mother wears hip boots in case she steps in a hole concealed beneath the water hyacinths. Living in the swamp has given the Cookes a large measure of self-sufficiency. At left, June gathers oyster mushrooms that sprout on willows and tupelo gums after a rain. They will flavor stews, soups, and meat dishes. At far left, Linda washes the skin of a nutria trapped by her husband, Pete. Raccoon skins hang nearby. At upper left, Pete trims June's hair on the porch of the family's cypress camp boat.

PRECEDING PAGES: Spanish moss drapes venerable cypress trees on Lake Verret. Though still abundant here, the moss has diminished in the swamp in recent years, its growth possibly impaired by air pollution or herbicides.

Droplets touched by early-morning sun sparkle on fluted, foot-wide lotus pads afloat on Lake Fausse Pointe. In such watery habitats, swamp life flutters, prowls, and hisses. A Gulf fritillary butterfly (far left) spreads gaudy wings of orange and silver; an immature yellow-crowned night heron, frozen by a spotlight, pauses in its quest for crawfish; and a cottonmouth, ready to strike, stands its ground.

Adirondacks

A Lived-In Wilderness, A Park for a Home

By Christine Eckstrom Lee
Photographs by Mark Godfrey

The moose was shot before anyone can remember. His massive head protrudes above the fireplace in the Adirondak Loj as if he had just poked in to have a look. Some people call him George. In George's commanding presence, the objects on the walls and mantel often pass unnoticed. Fading photographs, yellowed maps, deer antlers. A chunk of wood, a broken clock. Across the mantel and around the walls, the objects unfurl a running tale of the backcountry wilderness known as the Adirondacks.

Some of them are man-made, others are works of nature. The combination befits the region. For more than a century men and women have worked to preserve the natural beauty and wildness of the Adirondack Mountains in upstate New York. Although the area has been a state park for more than 85 years, the struggle to protect it continues today. Just hours from the most populous city in America, just a day's drive for tens of millions of eastern residents, America's largest park stands in delicate balance. In the Adirondacks, no place is more than ten miles from at least a dirt road. Yet a person can walk where hundreds have walked and still feel he is the first.

On a cold and drizzly October morning, photographer Mark Godfrey and I set out to climb Wright Peak, at 4,580 feet the 16th-highest Adirondack mountain. For three miles we wove with the trail through dense, wet forest that seemed to produce its own rain. At the spur trail that led half a mile to the summit, an ominous sign warned of the dangers higher up: unpredictable conditions, flash storms. We ate soggy sandwiches and decided to go on, up slippery rocks, over decomposing logs. As if we had stepped through the looking glass, the trees grew smaller, while we seemed to grow taller. Ahead, the wind rushed in long, shuddering moans, like music playing in a distant room. Trees creaked. Now and again the wind swooped

Still-life portrait from a land "forever wild," a glassy pond reflects the beauty of the Adirondack Park, a six-million-acre backcountry tract in upstate New York. It has preserved the area's mountains, lakes, and forests for nearly a century.

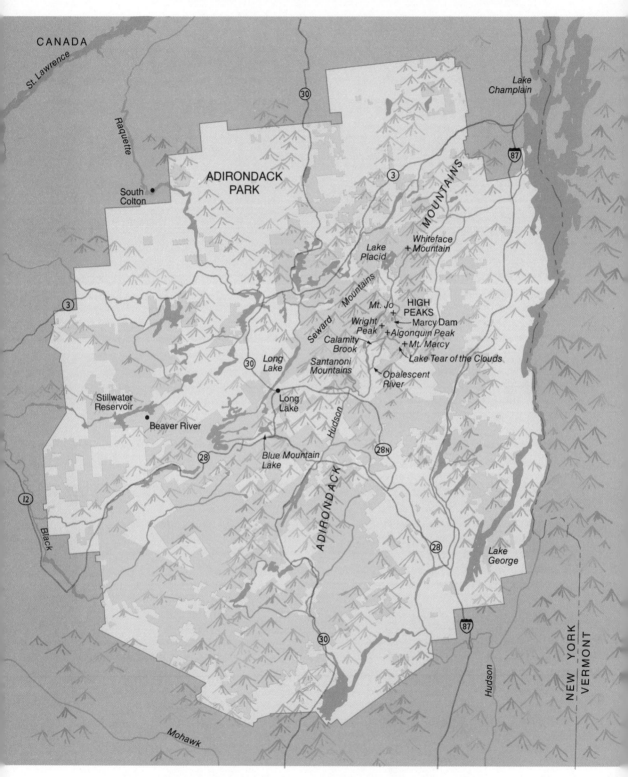

Adirondack Park, an area larger than Massachusetts, but with a
population one-fifth the size of Boston's. The Adirondack Park Agency,
formed in 1971, regulates use of both the public and private lands.

through the trail corridor, nudging us onward. We picked our way up a natural staircase of jumbled boulders and over a ledge where suddenly, in a clean line, the trees stopped. We stood up and a gust of wind punched us back like dazed boxers. Before us lay a hill of fissured rock, barren of protective trees. Spaced up the slope were cairns, neat pyramids of stones, marking the path to the top.

"You really want to do this?" Mark asked.

"It can't be very far. I think that's the last one," I said, pointing to a cairn. Obscured by a layer of fast-moving clouds, it faded in and out of visibility. Between blasts of wind, we tried to run from cairn to cairn, like soldiers dodging gunfire. Beyond the last one, another row of stone pyramids marched up yet another slope. I stood up to look. Whip! My hat was gone. The moment before, I had pulled it tight to shield my ears. Then, as if snatched by unseen hands, it flew from my head and dropped suddenly, a mere ten feet from where I stood. I was startled. And scared. I couldn't risk four steps to reach it. The next gust knocked me to my hands and knees, and my hat was swept from the mountain into the clouds.

One more cairn. And another. The wind whipped us like silk flags. Surrounded by dozens of splendid mountains, we saw nothing but white sky—and the next cairn. The mound of rock ahead arched like the back of a whale. No cairn marked its crest. The summit! Slowly, I crawled up the mound, pausing to crouch motionless, my head down. Slowly, I wobbled to my knees, eased to my feet, and stood up for a moment, arms outstretched, and screamed, *"We did it!"* My cry was sucked away in the wind.

Mark and I probably should have been more cautious when we hiked up Wright Peak. Several days later I visited the Atmospheric Sciences Research Center on nearby Whiteface Mountain. At noon on the day we had climbed Wright—just about the time we reached the summit—the winds there were gusting at 50 miles an hour. We were lucky. The Adirondacks can be as dangerous as the wild backcountry of Alaska. In June 1979, hikers spotted the wreckage of a small plane that had been lost in the Adirondacks since 1954.

If America's political lines followed the natural boundaries that define a region, there would probably be a State of Adirondack. Watercourses wreathe the area: Lake Champlain and Lake George to the east, the Mohawk and Hudson rivers to the south, the Black River and Lake Ontario to the west, the St. Lawrence River to the north. The land encircled by these waters is dense rolling forest spangled with lakes and streams. Five mountain ranges crosscut the region, and in the northeastern section mountains of the High Peaks Region rise to a crown.

The Adirondacks fall within the boundary lines of the State of New York. In turn, New York has drawn a boundary line around the Adirondacks, and named the land within the Adirondack Park. The park begins roughly 200 miles north of New York City, and extends toward Canada to embrace six million acres, home to 125,000 people. In the Adirondacks, a population one-fifth the size of Boston's lives in an area larger than Massachusetts.

On a magazine rack inside the lodge was a 1973 map of the Adirondacks that unfolded to a 4-by-5-foot rectangle. A thin blue line traced the perimeter of the park. Of the land within what is appropriately called the "blue line," 3.7 million acres are privately owned and 2.3 million acres are maintained by the state as a public forest preserve. The map is confusing. With the lines of 12 counties superimposed on odd-shaped green blocks of state forest, the park looks like a jigsaw puzzle of a jigsaw puzzle.

The story of the park is as checkered as its map. In 1885 the New York

Legislature established the forest preserve in the Adirondacks, and in 1892 it created the Adirondack Park. Two years later the New York Constitution was amended with a farsighted—and still controversial—clause. Little more than a year after the great Oklahoma land rush, in an era when few spoke of an end to America's wilderness, New Yorkers voted to keep the state's forest-preserve lands "forever wild." Most of those lands were in the Adirondacks. Decades of argument and legal interpretation have not diminished the ring of those words. Adirondack country is wild.

Like most Adirondack natives, Fred Burns is a master of many trades. He has built houses and a school, and worked at summer resorts and a power plant. In the last 25 years he has built his own home, a house next door for his nephews, a garage, and a two-story workshop, where he pursues his favorite arts: painting in oils and building guide boats. Several of his recent paintings line the walls, and the rib cage of his next boat is mounted on a long sawhorse stand in the center of the room. It will be his tenth. Adirondack guide boats are indigenous to the region; they evolved there, reaching aesthetic and practical perfection in the late 1800's. Sleek and low, they resemble a graceful cross between a rowboat and a canoe. The details of their construction would fill a volume, and the skill required to build one might rightfully be termed an art. Fred Burns fashions his boats in Long Lake style, the name of the village where he lives and of the lake the town overlooks. Fred came to Long Lake when he was 17. The year was 1909.

At 87, dressed in a red plaid shirt and hunter's cap, Fred is trim and spry and moves with the ease of a far younger man. He possesses a memory worthy of anyone's envy. He described to me a trip he had once made to California. He named the railroad lines and the places he stopped, describing the mountains and plains. "Then I come east," he said. "I got out at El Paso. Texas. That's when Black Jack Pershing was chasing Pancho Villa around. The town was full of soldiers. With .45's on their sides. But they didn't get Pancho." That year was 1916.

"Then the World War One come along." Fred enlisted in the Air Service of the U. S. Army, and when the war ended his friends asked about Long Lake. "Some of the boys in the service said, 'If we wanted to come see you, how would we get there?' Well, I said, starting from Grand Central Station, New York City, you go up to Albany and then west to Utica. You get off at Utica, take the Adirondack Division of the New York Central, ride another 90 miles and get out at Long Lake West. That's what they called it then, now they call it Sabattis. Somebody'll meet you there with a buckboard, two-seater. You get on and ride 19 miles to Long Lake. Then you get across the lake. I didn't tell about the bridge, I guess, so one fella says, 'When you get to Long Lake, you swim!'"

"Did anyone ever come?"

"No!" he laughed.

In that seemingly faraway time, the guide boat and guide were essential to travel in the Adirondacks. The route from here to there was usually along lakes and streams connected by overland portages, or "carries." The fashionable denizens of New York City who flocked to the Adirondacks in the late 1800's relied on the local guides to lead them on sporting adventures. Vanderbilts, Whitneys, Astors, Stuyvesants, Tiffanys, Biddles, four U. S. presidents, and a list of literary luminaries that would crowd a Who's Who all came to the Adirondacks to vacation and savor the wilderness.

Fred recounts the names of Long Lake boatmen in the same way a history student recites the names of presidents. "All the old boatbuilders are gone. But when I came to Long Lake 70 years ago, all the traveling was done in guide boats. Just like a cowboy would go a quarter of a mile this way to get his horse to ride half a mile that way. The guide boat was it."

A way of life has changed in Fred's lifetime—in Long Lake, in the Adirondacks, in the world. "Used to be a cow pasture where the school is. Cows used to roam from there down to the marsh until 'long toward spring. It was dry on that marsh till the thaws came, melted the snow. Cows used to feed there. Now I don't think there's one cow in town."

He looked out the window of his house. "Everything changed with the automobiles," he said. "From the old life I mean, that used to be." He looked up at me, his blue eyes glistening. "What next?"

I looked at him, empty-handed, and said I didn't know.

We loaded Fred's best guide boat on a two-wheel carrier and rolled it down the road from his house to Long Lake. The air was fresh and cold, the sky cloudless. It was the sort of autumn weather that turns a walk into a skip. The bright blue waters of Long Lake were calm, and near the shore the perfect reflection of red- and gold-leaved trees seemed painted on the surface. Fred hopped in his guide boat, pushed off from shore, and rowed, pulling the oars like a crewman. He executed some fancy maneuvers, dipping first one oar, then the other, turning with the grace of a dancer.

My turn. I sat down, feet braced against a wooden bar, and rocked from side to side, trying to balance the boat. Fred looked skeptical. "That's cold water. You ready for a swim?" He positioned the boat and gave it a push. At first, I flailed. The oars slapped and gouged the water; I seemed to go nowhere. From the air I must have resembled a wounded bird. Fred shouted instructions from the shore, and I began to catch on. The oars of an Adirondack guide boat overlap. I stroked slowly, crossing my hands over and under each other. I skinned my knuckles. "You get used to that," said Fred. Then, it worked. I glided across the water, fast and smooth. I had the sensation of being at once beneath the water and a part of its surface. Fred called from the shore, "You got it! You got it! That's it!"

Fred pulled the boat across the Long Lake bridge, toward the hill that leads to his house. We paused by the roadside while several cars whizzed by. One passed slowly, then stopped. Fred continued along the road.

"Hey!" someone shouted. I turned around. "Hey! Where'd you get that boat?" I looked at Fred, crossing the road with boat in tow. He hadn't heard. I looked back to the car. Three people had climbed out, stepping hesitantly forward. "Where can you rent those boats?" I answered the first question. "He made it." Fred kept walking. "Does he want to sell it?" I looked at Fred across the road, his head turned to the lake. "No." I smiled and waved. As they shut the car doors, Fred turned around. "What was that?" The car revved away from a swirl of gravel dust. "They wanted to buy your boat." Still walking, he smiled and shook his head.

To the Mohawk tribe of upstate New York and the Algonquin Indians of Canada, who roamed the woods before white men came, the Adirondacks were a hunting and trapping ground. They probably never settled in the region. Furs were the lure that led to the first Adirondack boom. Beaver abounded in the region, and their pelts were highly prized. Beginning in the late 17th century, trappers ranged over the area, and by the mid-1800's the beavers were nearly gone.

Pioneers passed the Adirondacks by. After the American Revolution, a few Vermont farmers trickled into the area, and wrested a rugged life from the rocky soil. When the Erie Canal opened in the 1820's, nearly everyone skirted the Adirondacks, bound for the rich lands farther west.

As early as 1810, another resource was discovered and exploited: iron. Miners sought fortunes from the rich Adirondack iron veins. A few succeeded, many failed. But until the 1870's, the Adirondacks supplied the bulk of the iron used in the eastern United States.

The cry of "Timber!" characterized yet another boom in the Adirondacks in the early 1800's. Lumbermen in a wood-hungry nation were quick to realize that, although there was no gold in the hills, the Adirondacks were themselves a gold mine of timber. They bought vast tracts of land, logged the forests, and became a powerful lobbying force.

But the lumbermen weren't alone in the Adirondack hills. The "rusticators"—sportsmen and hikers, artists and naturalists—all began to discover the mountains. Like the lumbermen, wealthy families bought thousands of acres, and along wooded lakeshores they built their camps. "Camp" is a modest word, but in the Adirondacks its definition "went to seed and ran wild," writes Adirondack historian Alfred L. Donaldson. "If you have spent the night in a guide's tent, or a lean-to built of slabs and bark, you have lodged in a 'camp.' If you chance to know a millionaire, you may be housed in a cobblestone castle, tread on Persian rugs, bathe in a marble tub . . . and still your host may call his mountain home a 'camp.'"

But the area was being overused. The forests were ringing with the sound of axes, and fires—often ignited by sparks from locomotives—were burning in the logging areas. Streams and rivers were drying up, threatening New York City's water supply and endangering downstate canals. Soon a cry arose: "Save the woods!" The rusticators and other interested men and women joined together to try to preserve the wilderness. As early as 1857, journalist Samuel H. Hammond wrote, "Civilization is pushing its way even toward this wild and, for all agricultural purposes, sterile region, and before many years even the Rackett [River] will be within its ever-extending circle. When that time shall have arrived, where shall we go to find the woods, the wild things, the old forests. . . . Had I my way, I would mark out a circle of a hundred miles in diameter, and throw around it the protecting aegis of the constitution. I would make it a forest forever."

Hammond's plea was visionary. In 1894, the New York Constitution was amended to read, "The lands of the State, now owned or hereafter acquired, constituting the forest preserve as now fixed by law, shall be forever kept as wild forest lands. They shall not be leased, sold or exchanged, or be taken by any corporation, public or private, nor shall the timber thereon be sold, removed or destroyed." A conservation movement was born in the Adirondacks, and steps were taken to repair the land. Trees were planted, lakes were restocked with fish, and at the turn of the century beaver were reintroduced. They thrived.

The chunk of wood on the mantel of the lodge is gnawed to a pencil-sharp point at each end, the work of an industrious beaver. Beavers increased so successfully that by 1940 trapping them was once again permitted. Their dams barricade many a stream in the Adirondacks, creating ponds that slowly change to bogs, spongy ground with the consistency of setting gelatin. In time, the bogs become solid enough for spruce seedlings and other plants to sprout, and the land becomes forest. But somewhere else a new pond is forming, as beavers build another dam.

In his log workshop outside South Colton, a town near the northwestern border of the Adirondack Park, Bill Smith sells a variety of traps and lures. Neatly arrayed, they hang from one wall like harp strings, in ascending order of size. Muskrat and mink, fisher and fox, otter and beaver. All roam the region; there is a trap for (Continued on page 133)

"Transportation meant guide boats when I came to Long Lake 70 years ago," says Fred Burns, one of a handful of craftsmen who still build them. "Some builders make their boats narrow for racing," he says, "but who wants to race all the time?"

dirondack autumn: Vivid birch, beech, and maple trees flame among evergreens on

*the shores of Long Lake. In the distance, snow dusts peaks of the Seward
Mountains. A clamorous honking fills the air, then fades, as a wedge of migrating
Canada geese wings southward. Calamity Brook (left) mirrors the season.*

*W*oodcraft in the Adirondacks: Outdoorsman Bill Smith
*hunts, traps, teaches, buys furs, sells supplies—and fashions
traditional Adirondack pack baskets, used for carrying
provisions and trappers' supplies. Shoulder straps hold the
baskets snugly on the backs of woodsmen. "The Indians
taught me to make baskets when I was a boy," he explains.
"Now I can't keep up with the demand for them." Inside a
log workshop he built, Bill puts the finishing touches on a*

basket (below). From beginning to end, basketmaking requires both strength and patience. At left, Bill separates layers of wood from a black ash log; pounding with the blunt end of an ax loosens the cut layers—each a strip of an annual growth ring. After trimming and smoothing the strips, he weaves the basket (opposite, below). His skills make Bill typical of the old-time inhabitants of the Adirondacks. In their isolation they had to make, grow, find, or hunt virtually everything they needed. That spirit of self-reliance continues in a region where traditional skills and values remain important. "But pretty near everything I do," Bill muses, "is a dying art."

Woodland pond rises behind a beaver dam in the Adirondacks. Beginning in the 1600's, the fashion for men's hats of beaver fur fueled an insatiable demand for the animals. Ranging ever farther in search of them, trappers began exploring in and around the area. By the late 1800's, only about a dozen beavers remained in the Adirondacks. Alarmed, the state legislature passed a law to protect them. Conservationists brought beavers from as far away as Wyoming and released them in the Adirondacks. They thrived, and today maintain such a healthy population that game laws permit trapping in certain areas. Around the base of a birch felled by the animals (opposite, below) lies a litter of wood chips. A pond created by a beaver dam at first kills trees by drowning their roots; later, as aquatic plants invade, die, and sink to the bottom, the pond gradually disappears and trees return.

FOLLOWING PAGES: Young tamarack trees, turning yellow in autumn, spring up around the boggy edges of a shrinking Adirondack pond.

*L*and of raw and subtle beauty: From the rushing waters of the Opalescent River (left) to the delicate palette of autumn color formed by fallen leaves (below), the Adirondack wilderness continues to inspire artists, as it has for more than a century. His paint box slung over his shoulder (right), artist Don Wynn heads for his home near Blue Mountain Lake. Nineteenth-century painters of the Hudson River School first captured the romance of the Adirondack wilds. Their canvases helped whet the public appetite for untamed lands—a public that later encouraged protection of the Adirondacks.

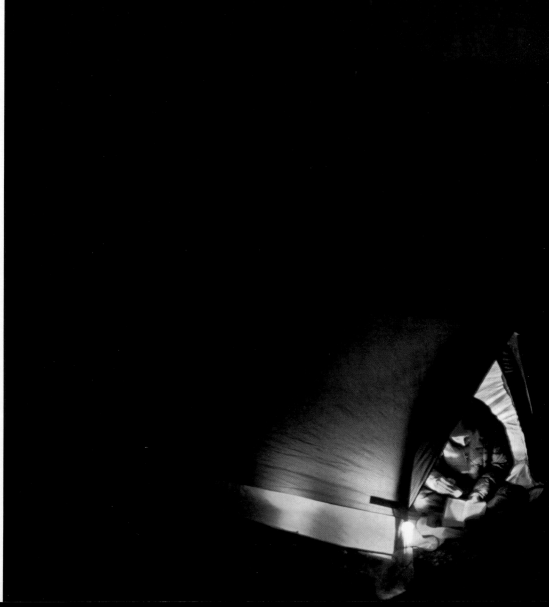

Candlelit tent atop Mount Jo shelters author Chris Eckstrom Lee (left) as sunlight fades beyond a dark ridge. "We camped on Mount Jo simply for the beauty of the view— and the solitude," she says. Frosty trees fringe the summit ledge where she sets up her tent (top). As the afternoon sun dipped lower, the thermometer dropped steadily. "By the time I began cooking supper," she recalls, "the temperature was below freezing. I didn't have to move my hand to stir the eggs: I just held the spoon in the pan and shivered."

*R*aw gusts buffet the author as she scrambles through fog and driving rain above the timberline on Wright Peak. "I had to stick close to the rock," she says, "using my hands almost as much as my feet. At times, I was afraid the wind would actually sweep me off the mountain." The lure of mountaintops draws countless hikers to the Adirondacks each year. Above, the author stands erect for an exultant moment atop the 4,580-foot peak.

each. Bill is a trapper, but like Fred Burns he suffers no lack of occupations. He is also a teacher, hunter, tanner, maker of pack baskets, and licensed guide. Trapping and fur-buying account for about a third of his income. Arranged in rows on his workshop floor were the results of his recent trapping efforts: six muskrats, two minks, a raccoon, and a red fox.

Bill's face is lined and tan, and he speaks in a lilting rhythm, pronouncing words like "guide" as "goyd," "nice" as "noyce." At 41, he has accumulated a lifetime's knowledge of woodcraft. I once said to him, "If I were dropped from the sky into this wilderness . . ."

"You'd die," he said. "I'd survive. Now I could maybe go to the desert and not make out so good. I'm sure I could make it, but I wouldn't live as high on the hog as I would up here."

Bill knows animals. From clues they leave in the woods, he reconstructs entire scenarios of what animals do—and why. "There's a place up on Chap Hill where I found a black cherry tree right over a deer trail, and underneath there was all these pieces of bark on the ground. My friend and I got to looking and we decided a bobcat had been out on that limb. You could see where he laid there, and he kneaded that limb, you know how they do with their claws, just like a house cat. And he'd taken the outer bark off that limb waiting for a deer to come. We got to looking and we found a dead doe about 80 yards up the trail. That bobcat had caught that doe and killed it, and had it all covered with leaves."

Bill traps and hunts to feed his family. "When it comes meat time, I go out and get my deer." He understands and respects each animal's niche. One night he set a trap for a fox. In the morning the bait was gone, the trap upside-down. "This happened four or five nights in a row. The fox kept flipping the trap and stealing the bait. I got to thinking, if I set this trap bottom side up, that fox'll flip it over and I'll catch him.

"So I did and I caught the fox. It was a female, and I let her go. I thought, if you're that smart I'm gonna let you go. Sometimes the animals make such a fool of you, you wonder who's outsmarting who."

Photographer Mark Godfrey and I went along with Bill to see his trapline. "I checked 'em this morning," he said. "But we'll have a look just in case." He brought his gun. "Let me know if you see any partridges; I'll take 'em home," he said. We bounced along a dirt road in his station wagon, through the wooded land where his traps were set. "A trapper has to be a conservationist or he won't survive," he said. "He has to know the woods, the tracks, the animals." We stopped near a trap. Nothing. "I've caught hunters before, by the fingers. Doesn't hurt 'em, really. You can see where some guy was walking along and said, 'What's that?' He goes over and investigates. Some of 'em take their fingers and start digging in there. Well, they get caught. So they put the trap down, put a foot on each spring, and pull their fingers out. They probably do it faster than that, too. You can see what they did by what's left. In one case I found the trap way over in the woods. I could almost hear the guy swearing when he threw it."

He stopped the car. "There's a partridge right there. See it?" I looked and looked and saw only branches and leaves. Bill picked up his gun and jumped out of the car. Quickly he dropped in a shell and aimed. Boom! He retrieved the bird, and brought it to the car. "There's always a little lunch laying around for you somewhere," he said. He held out the partridge to

Chill waters of the Opalescent River glow golden early on a September morning. Tumbling down the slopes of Mount Marcy, the Opalescent soon joins water flowing from Lake Tear of the Clouds—highest source of the Hudson River. 133

me. "It's a female, see this feather right here? Doesn't have a black stripe on it." He turned the bird gently in his hands. "A clean shot. We'll have it for lunch tomorrow."

The traps were empty, and we returned to his house. "One of the local guys is coming by with a bear," he said. "Have you ever seen a bear?"

"Only in the zoo. I've worried about them a lot, in the woods."

"They won't hurt you. Some people feed 'em right out of their hands, but I'm not one of those. Someday somebody's gonna get between a mother and her cubs, and if they do they're gonna get batted upside the head and that'll be the end of 'em. Some of those old sows weigh four or five hundred pounds, and boy, they rap you and you know it."

"That's what I'm worried about."

"They'll leave you alone if you leave them alone. I've been over back picking berries before, and the bears'll be on the other side of the patch picking berries. You just keep an eye on them. They won't bother you."

"Have you ever shot a bear?"

"I shot one once. I'd never shoot another. I don't think there's enough around here anymore. Bear meat's good, a young one's good. Tastes something like a combination between pork and beef. This guy coming here, he wants the skin. That's all he wants. He killed it yesterday, first day of hunting season." Soon a truck wheeled into Bill's driveway; a man jumped out to talk to him. Bill's family, Mark, and I all gathered at the rear of the truck to see the bear. She lay on her side as if she were asleep; her rich black fur shone blue in the sun.

"She's a beautiful bear," said Bill. "Pretty big one, too," said the man. "Three hundred twenty pounds." "They get bigger," said Bill. We all stared at the bear. Bill rubbed her fur. "You ever felt bear fur?" he said to me. "Feel how soft she is." I ran my hand across her fur. It was thick and silky. "This your first bear?" he asked the man. "Yeah, probably my last one. It was a lot more trouble than I thought." Bill checked the bear's teeth, spread her paws. "Why did you shoot her?" he asked. "Did she charge?" "No," said the man. "She was eating berries in the bushes." "So why did you shoot her?" Bill repeated. "Just for the sake of it, I guess." The man looked around, at the bushes, the road, his feet.

"I wanted to get a bear."

Mark and I wandered away from the truck, leaving them to talk. Soon the man drove away. "I told him I didn't have time to skin it," Bill said. "I got too many things to do as it is."

He put his hands in his pockets and looked down the road. "He doesn't want that bear. He shot it, and now he doesn't know what to do with it. He can't skin it, he doesn't want the meat. You can't do that. Trapping fox and shooting bears is like harvesting potatoes or anything else. You just take what you need, and you always leave seed for the next year. You have to leave seed, that's how it goes on."

The Adirondacks have always attracted people with a zest for self-sufficiency, and part of the region's enduring appeal is that a life away from the mainstream can be found by those who seek it. If I were a hermit deciding to make a gradual return to civilization, the first place I would settle would be Beaver River, the most isolated village in New York. On a rainy October day, Mark and I visited the town.

We arrived by floatplane on the Stillwater Reservoir, whose flooding in the twenties severed Beaver River's only road link to the outside world. Near the reservoir, a row of old cars rested in deep grass. Most were a welded amalgam of models and colors, lacking such decorative accessories as bumpers, door handles, lights, and mirrors. Some had shattered windshields, some were only half there, like sawed-off shotguns. Not one had a license plate. Yet what seemed to be a junkyard was in fact a parking lot. The residents of Beaver River bring in old cars by barge, and use them to carry supplies from the reservoir into town. As the town has no electricity, residents must haul in bottled gas and kerosene for fuel. From the reservoir, a single lane runs into town. The other roads in the town end abruptly in the woods; you can't leave the area by car. In Beaver River, where all roads lead to Beaver River, it is easy to understand why residents see no need for licenses for their vehicles.

Mark and I walked along the mile of sandy road leading from the reservoir into town. Only one building showed signs of life, the Norridgewock III hotel. It was a hunter's lodge at that time of year, clean and warm with a crackling fire. A jukebox stood in one corner; two young men played billiards, and the sound of rock music and the aroma of bacon emanated from the kitchen. Everything we saw seemed to belie Beaver River's remoteness on the map. Stan and Pat Thompson, the owners, talked with us as we sipped hot coffee at the dining room bar.

"You have to be a jack-of-all-trades to live in this town," said Stan. When the Thompsons' lodge burned to the ground in 1973, there was nothing they could do to save it. Beaver River has no fire department; in fact, it has no water or sewer system. But with help from friends, the Thompsons rebuilt the hotel in less than two months. They reared their five children in Beaver River. Pat taught school in the town for six years, obtaining books and course materials through a University of Maryland program. "Educating children in a remote area is difficult," she said. "But when most of the students are your own children, it's even harder!"

There are no children in Beaver River now. Its year-round population is 12. "Will you stay here to live?" I asked Rusty Thompson, Stan and Pat's son, as he drove Mark and me back to the reservoir in one of Beaver River's unusual automobiles. "I'm not sure yet," he said. "Sometimes it's too quiet and lonely here. My folks call Beaver River the 'Outback of the Adirondacks.' I think it's true. When the train service stopped in 1965, we got snowmobiles. Otherwise the only way to get here in the winter is by snowshoes or skis." The only way to get to Beaver River during the remainder of the year is by foot, boat, or floatplane.

In the winter, the trails around Beaver River buzz with snowmobiles, and the Thompson's hotel is filled with vacationing families. In spring and summer, hikers visit the area; in fall, the hunters arrive. Despite its small population, Beaver River isn't empty; and with the improvised comforts the Thompsons have brought to their home, their life seems almost suburban. "It's beautiful here," Pat had told me. "But it's not an easy life. The sense of isolation is always ominously present."

In the distance, we heard the low drone of Herb Helms's floatplane. He landed on the reservoir, taxied to the dock, and flew Mark and me back to Long Lake. For 32 years, Herb has operated his small floatplane business in Long Lake, not far from where Fred Burns lives. Soft-spoken and calm, Herb flies tourists, hunters, and fishermen over the High Peaks and into the woods for backcountry pleasure trips. He knows the shape of every Adirondack peak and pond from the air. At sunset on an autumn day, we flew above Mount Marcy, 5,344 feet high, the Everest of the Adirondacks. Herb banked the plane and circled the mountains. Lake Tear of the Clouds, the highest source of the Hudson River, gleamed silver on Marcy's shoulder. A sea of mountains surrounds Marcy, rolling to the horizon like storm waves. "I never get tired of looking at them," Herb said.

From the air, the Adirondacks seem an unpeopled wilderness. The forest presses close to the shores of lakes and the edges of towns. The evidence of people—cleared patches of land, tiny threads of roads—is small and faint. It seems that, if the towns and roads were left untended, the Adirondacks could easily swallow it all.

The Adirondack Park, however, is a lived-in wilderness. Concern for the overuse of public lands, coupled with fears about the future development of private holdings, led to the creation in 1971 of the Adirondack Park Agency. As an overseeing body for the entire region, the Park Agency produced two master plans for the use of public and private lands in the park. State land has been divided into areas ranging from "wilderness" to "travel corridors," their uses carefully defined. Permits must be obtained and approved for any improvements to private land that affect the entire region, and density regulations have been established.

Robert Frost once wrote of America and its people, "The land was ours before we were the land's." With regard to the Park Agency, many an Adirondack native might express the reverse of that thought: "We are the land's but now it is not ours." They sense a betrayal of trust, and the future of the Park Agency will hinge, in part at least, on its ability to work out problems with the people who live in the park now, have lived there for generations, will always live there.

The formation of the Park Agency was a landmark decision, destined to influence the Adirondacks as surely as the "forever wild" amendment did nearly a century ago. What that impact will be is uncertain, but for now the land is protected.

With deference normally reserved for heroes, the Adirondacks have a monument to timelessness and datelessness. It is known as Sunday Rock. When it was officially dedicated in 1925, Dr. Charles Leete proclaimed its importance: "Be it then known to all people that Sunday Rock is a glacial boulder of towering form standing high alongside the road to the South Woods, or the Adirondack wilderness. . . . And it is called Sunday Rock because in days of old . . . it was said that beyond this rock there was no Sunday. . . . There were no days by any names. . . . The river, the brooks, the ponds, the mountains, and the trees, the fleet deer, the rushing trout, the wild cat and bear ruled supreme. It was their land and there was no Sunday there."

In the shadow of George the moose's palmate antlers, a clock rests on the mantel of the Adirondak Loj. It is a handsome wooden clock with Arabic numerals; the hands always read 9:40. John Stacey, the manager, set the hands there deliberately. "It's a nice time, day or night," he explains. "Not too early, not too late. People come here to relax. They don't want to think about the time and the date and their jobs in the city. They're here to get away from those things."

As his floatplane bobbed on the waters of Long Lake, Herb Helms had said to me, "There really haven't been many changes here. We've had people come here who haven't been to the Adirondacks for a number of years and who say, 'Why, it's just the same, it's just as I remembered it.' That's what the visitors want, and in a sense that's what we want, too."

This year, visitors will return to the Adirondacks, to their favorite mountains, favorite lakes, and find them as they were last year, as they were ten or a hundred years ago. And ten or a hundred years from now, perhaps people will find them the same.

Fallen leaves crunch underfoot as the snow-sprinkled summit trail on Mount Jo beckons a backpacker onward. The open vistas of autumn—when trees free of foliage permit a longer view—tempt hikers prepared to cope with wind and cold.

*S*nows of October whiten the Santanoni Mountains. Mount Marcy, at 5,344 feet
the highest mountain in New York, stands on the horizon to the right of center.
More than 40 summits rise above 4,000 feet in this northeastern section of the park—
the High Peaks Region. Climbing on Mount Marcy began in 1837, when local guide
John Cheney led a survey party to its summit. "It makes a man feel what it is to
have all creation placed beneath his feet," he said, describing his feelings at the
summit. Upon scaling 46 of the loftiest peaks, climbers earn the distinction of
becoming "Adirondack Forty-Sixers." At left, hoarfrost filigrees leaves and grasses.

Winter fun in the Adirondacks means slipping and sliding, snowy tumbles and helping hands—or poles. Cross-country skiers (left) make poor time down a forested trail in the High Peaks Region. Above, the author stands still for a checkup: fellow skier Susan McElhinney scrapes accumulated snow and ice from her skis. Icicles grow in the beard of Peter Swain, and John Stacey provides a perch for a black-capped chickadee lured by bits of bread.

As evening falls, cross-country skiers glide along a trail through a grove of snow-shrouded red pines. Below, they ski on Marcy Dam pond. Throughout the seasons, the Adirondack Park offers a variety of backcountry recreational opportunities. Just a day's drive for millions of Americans, it holds few, if any, unexplored places; even its most remote point lies less than ten miles from a road of sorts. Yet a sense of wilderness remains. Since the enactment of a farsighted amendment to the state constitution in 1894, the park's forestlands have remained wild. "You can step a stone's throw from the road," says the author, "walk where hundreds have walked, and still feel that you are the first."

Death Valley

The Grandeur of Life
In a Stark Desert World

By Cynthia Russ Ramsay
Photographs by Paul Chesley

Anything could happen in a land of such extremes—the driest desert, the highest temperatures, and the lowest elevation in North America. And, according to the old-timers, almost everything did. Take, for example, the tale a prospector told some 50 years ago about the blazing heat of Death Valley.

"I had my boorows loaded with bags a corn. It was in July . . . and the valley was so hot that the corn started poppen and all the bags busted open. That corn scattered all over and kept on poppen until they was a big pile a white popcorn all around me. My fool boorows thought them white heaps was snow and they laid down in the sand and froze to death."

Other tales, not all of them exaggerations, tell of lost mines and hidden treasures, terrible suffering and violent deeds.

I pondered such things one bright December morning as I drove to Death Valley National Monument in Nevada and eastern California, on the northern fringe of the Mojave Desert. A turnoff from the main road from Las Vegas led me to Dantes View, a mile-high overlook in the Black Mountains on the eastern rim of the valley. From there I gazed down upon a long, narrow basin, much of it encrusted with salt, startling in its whiteness. Two parallel mountain ranges rise abruptly from the valley floor and lock the land between massive walls of rock endowed with a splendor of color—russet and rose, magenta and mustard yellow, amber and apricot. Countless gullies and crevices, crags and ridges cast long, sharp shadows—black streaks that underline the gaunt contours of the landscape.

Ahead, the Panamint Range soars so high its summits are mantled with snow; down below, centuries of ferocious heat have baked an ancient lake to salt. The view carries my eyes from 11,049-foot Telescope Peak, the highest point in the range, down to 282 feet below sea level.

The only sound is that of the wind, moaning as it rushes down the

Salt whitens the floor of Death Valley, a sere basin that stretches for 150 miles in the Mojave Desert. Golden clumps of hardy desert speargrass grow at Dantes View. The distant Panamint Range rises beyond the stark valley floor.

slopes and sweeps across the level emptiness of the desert. Fleecy clouds, chased by the wind, dapple the harsh glitter of the salt flats with their shadows. It is a scene of stark, intimidating beauty, with vegetation too sparse to blur or grace the immensity of stone, salt, and sky. Everything has a hard edge, even the moaning wind.

I look for water and see none, though I know that just out of sight below me is a bitter, briny pool with an appropriate if unimaginative name: Badwater. No rivers flow from the canyons that cut through the rock. They run with water only after heavy rains. Instead, great slopes of gravel, sand, and silt fan out from the mouths of the dry canyons, burying the lower flanks of the mountains and spilling onto the valley floor.

My very first hike teaches me that distance distorts the steepness and size of these fans, for aeons of flash floods have spewed forth enough debris to make the largest of them several miles long and half a mile thick.

Distance, I discover, also diminishes the beauty and fascination of Death Valley. To get to know a land where seeds lie dormant for years awaiting sufficient rainfall to sprout, where some of the flowers are pinhead small, where camouflage blends much of the wildlife into the landscape, where rocks change color with every hour of the day—all this takes time, and it takes sturdy hiking boots. For Death Valley reserves many of its wonders for those who set out to explore its vastness on foot.

A few weeks in Death Valley is plenty of time to feel its desert calm, to find flowers blooming in the crevices of canyon walls, and to watch lizards disappearing under rocks. But ordinarily such a brief visit is insufficient for the understanding that brings true wonder. So I am indebted to the people who accompanied photographer Paul Chesley and me on our excursions into the backcountry; without them we would have seen less, and understood less, of what makes Death Valley such an awesome, beautiful place.

Paul and I made Furnace Creek our headquarters. There the National Park Service has a visitor center, and hotels and restaurants have also claimed this oasis in the center of the valley.

Paul proved to have many admirable talents. With his photographer's eye, he could spot a burro on a distant hillside or an interesting rock in a pile of rubble. He could pinpoint our location, quickly and easily matching the brown contour lines on the topographic maps to the scenery. But most important, he could cook and season trail food to perfection.

We talked Park Ranger Dan Dellinges into joining us for a three-day backpacking trip into the Panamints. Slender but obviously very strong, Dan has spent many of his 26 years outdoors. He prefers to hike alone. "I like to be out in the desert where there's nobody ahead of me and nobody behind me," he told us.

Our four-wheel-drive van crunched down an unpaved road on the west side of the valley to the base of the fan below Six Spring Canyon, and before long we were hiking up its unshaded length under a cloudless, shining sky. The slope, which had looked like a desolation of rock from a distance, was actually studded with low, widely spaced clumps of desert holly, a shrub with silver-gray leaves that were softly luminescent in the slanting morning light. Of the more than 600 species of plants that grow within the boundaries of the monument, none, I think, evokes the desert better than this shrub that looks so dainty, yet remains stubbornly alive in the hottest and driest part of the gravel fan. The desert holly has a formidable strategy for survival. The salt it absorbs from the soil gives its leaves a pale color that, by reflecting sunlight, apparently helps keep the plant cool. The leaves, leathery to the touch, may curl up in summer to escape the full impact of the sun. And in the driest times, the plant drops some of its leaves until its next drink.

Since a plant can lose as much as 95 percent of its moisture through its leaves, many Death Valley species have developed defenses against dehydration. Some plants have fuzzy leaves covered with fine hairs that reflect sunlight and provide a barrier against the drying wind. Many have very small leaves, and most cactus plants have no leaves at all.

The creosote bush, which thrives in this land of little rain and brutal heat, grows very slowly. It matures and reaches maximum height within a few decades but continues spreading from its original stem to form a circle of satellite shrubs. In some places, these circles reach a diameter of 60 feet, which means that the original plant began growing hundreds of years ago.

No such Methuselah appeared along our route, but I proposed a halt, more to seek the scant shade of the creosote bush than to rest. By this time we had shed our jackets and were sweating in short sleeves. Heat rose from the gravel. It beat down from the sky. And this was December!

We had been hiking for more than two hours. Our vehicle was a dot in the distance, and still the fan swept upward toward the mouth of the canyon. A broad expanse of creosote bushes stretched before us.

We stopped again while Paul tried to edge closer to three burros that had been staring at us as we hiked by. Descendants of animals lost or abandoned by miners and prospectors, burros in the monument number about 1,800 now, thriving on such scraggly, twiggy shrubs as Mormon tea and boxthorn. As Paul got closer, the burros would move a few feet away, then stop and turn back to look at him, waiting utterly still until he ventured forward again. Finally, perhaps wearying of the game, they trotted away.

As we approached the mouth of the canyon, we made use of the trails trampled by burros plodding between water holes. This made for easier walking, but we had to pick our way around their droppings, which were everywhere on the trails. Also, the animals had so fouled the streams and springs that nearly all were unsafe for drinking.

The higher we climbed, the larger and more robust the plants became. Water is the controlling factor, and precipitation increases with elevation. At Furnace Creek, on the valley floor, rainfall averages less than two inches a year; at 5,000 feet, the average rises to about six inches—enough to turn the creosote plants a vibrant green. It also induces such remarkable growth that I did not recognize the shoulder-high rabbit-brush as the same species I had seen in its smaller version below.

We followed a trail that snaked up the canyon, the sinuous curves of its walls shaped by the meanders of a river gone dry. We walked from sunlight to shade and back to sunlight again, alternating sweat with shivers of cold. Where the canyon opened into a valley, we set up camp. Since we had brought no tents, we simply kicked away some rocks and smoothed out places for our sleeping bags. Because it was winter, the mountains around us had melted into the darkness by six o'clock, so I wriggled down into the warmth of my sleeping bag. Long before dawn, however, I discovered that 12 hours of darkness makes for a very long night.

Our destination the second day was Hungry Bill's Ranch, a lush haven of green at the head of Johnson Canyon. In 1875 the high price of fresh food in the silver-mining town of Panamint City—cabbages, for example, brought $1.20 a head—lured Swiss farmers to this fertile patch of ground to grow vegetables, fruits, and nuts for the miners. Watered by snow that melts down from the crests in the spring, the trees still bring a harvest of apples, almonds, and walnuts to autumn hikers.

We had trudged up the saddle that separated us from Johnson Canyon, gloated over our speed, gazed at the panorama of peaks, and were trundling along up Johnson Canyon when we had a surprise. Rain! We had no tent, and I had been so zealous in reducing the weight of my pack that I had left my poncho behind. We found a shelter of sorts beneath a narrow ledge and warded off the gloom with Paul's dinner and mugs of hot chocolate. With the rain and the coming of night, it was soon dark. Wedged against the rock, I dropped off to sleep when the rain finally stopped. Then something skittered across my shoulder, and my shouts shattered the serenity of the desert night. With superb reflexes, both Dan and Paul were instantly awake, shouting too, and flailing about, proving once again that there's no way to get out of a sleeping bag in a hurry.

When the noise finally subsided, we established that we were not under attack and fished out our flashlights. Pack rats had been feasting on the food we had been too cold, wet, and lazy to put away, leaving an apple half-gnawed and bread nibbled to crumbs. Through the remainder of the night I listened vigilantly to the pack rats twittering and scurrying about. They were obviously indignant at our intrusion.

"You were trespassing! That rock shelter was their home," exclaimed Matt Ryan when I told him later about the pack rats. Matt has explored nearly all of the two million acres of the national monument. He came to Death Valley in 1942 as a laborer, later served here as a ranger, and finally retired in 1972 as superintendent of a park in Arizona. He returns regularly to the desert he still calls home. "Once you get this sand in your shoes, it's pretty hard to shake out," he explains.

Over the years Matt has seen the land mete out dreadful punishment to those careless of its dangers. "Most everybody I ever picked up dead or suffering from dehydration had a half-full canteen or had been close to water. One fellow died in the shade of his car with a case of soda pop in the trunk. Dehydration quickly affects the mind, and then there's a tendency to save whatever liquid you have, because you think you're going to need it later. The thing to do is to keep sipping to keep your ability to reason."

With Matt and his wife, Rosemary, we were on our way to the old Inyo gold mine, which had prospered back in the thirties and forties. As we drove the rough jeep road climbing Echo Canyon in the Funeral Mountains, Matt stopped frequently so we could look at the plants that, along with the ubiquitous creosote bush and desert holly, defied the lean, harsh land. Clumps of bunch grass sprouted on the mountainside like pale porcupines. Spiny barrels of cottontop cactus grew from toeholds high on the canyon walls. Desert trumpets, dried to a deep red, lifted their tapering stalks above the gravel. The gray leaves of a Death Valley sage seemed to spring from rock, and when I bent down for a close look at the shrub, which grows only in Death Valley, I found flecks of deep violet—tiny, color-charged blossoms half-hidden at the base of downy leaves.

"Flowers in December?"

But Matt explained that many desert plants ignore the calendar, and bloom whenever conditions of moisture and temperature are right. Sometimes this means a wait of many years. "Look at the variety of shapes and textures—all the different colors and patterns. It's all here if you learn to focus on small things and to observe details," Matt continued.

So, with eyes on the ground, we found the stingbush, paper-bag bush, brittlebush, and sandpaper plant, all appropriately named. The bleak desert had become a botanical garden (Continued on page 165)

Abandoned mill attests to the boom-and-bust history of gold mining in Death Valley. Matt Ryan, who retired from the National Park Service in 1972, tells a visitor of "the dreamers who poured in, lured by tales of lost mines and fabulous strikes."

"*I've been banging around this country for 40 years, but this time I've hit the mother lode,*" *says George Novak, a pick-and-shovel prospector who believes he has struck high-grade veins of silver in the Panamint Range. With a miner's glass, he looks for mineral traces in the rock. Silver nuggets he has extracted from ore glitter in his home; the rattles he finds more easily. Silver mining began in the Death Valley area in 1873, when a strike spawned wild and wide-open*

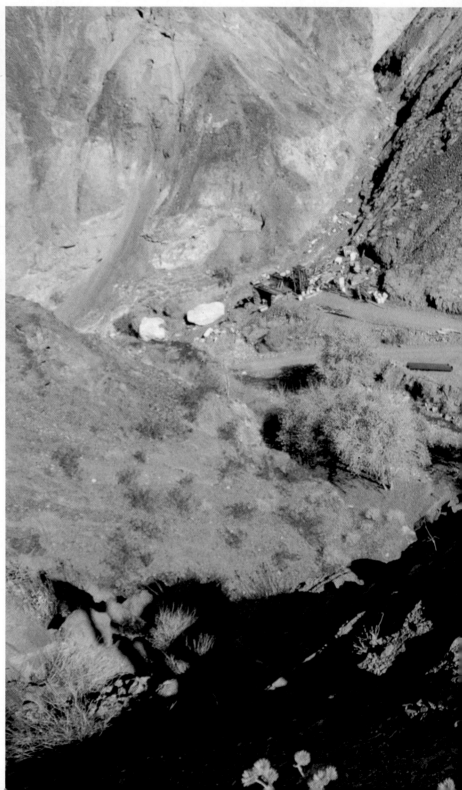

Panamint City. Later, discoveries of gold, copper, lead, and borax brought prospectors and miners to the region. Four companies, mining talc and borates, continue to operate in Death Valley National Monument, but a 1976 law prevents new claims.

FOLLOWING PAGES: Sunrise paints the sharply eroded clay ridges of the Zabriskie Point badlands. In such naked hills, sudden cloudbursts bring runoff and flash floods that strip the land.

Gnarled skeleton of a desert holly just a foot high (above) spreads scraggly branches against a stark landscape. At right, a shallow salt marsh collects both surface runoff and groundwater that seeps up from below the salt pan. Rubble washed out of the mountains by aeons of downpours spreads from a canyon in a gigantic alluvial fan (opposite). At the mouth of the canyon, the debris covers the valley floor with a deposit half a mile thick. Desert shrubs dot the gullied fan.

156

*B*arrels of a cottontop cactus bristle in Echo Canyon, and
pale desert holly clings to the rocky slopes. More than 600
species of plants grow in Death Valley National Monument,
in spite of ground temperatures as high as 190° F and
scant or salty water. Woolly leaves of the turtleback (right),
abloom in December with tiny yellow flowers, protect the
plant from desiccating winds. A young burro thrives in the
wild, eating the desert's shrubs and grasses. A scorpion
flexes its stinger, poised to defend itself with venom.

157

On the track of long-vanished mammals, author Cynthia Russ Ramsay (above, in sunglasses) joins geology students and their bearded professor, Fred Bachhuber, for a two-day field trip into the Black Mountains. There Dr. Bachhuber points out the fossilized tracks of a large cat, a camel, and a horse in a slab of shale. According to paleontologists, the creatures left their footprints on a mudflat about five million years ago. In time, the ooze hardened to rock, earthquakes lifted and tilted the land, and erosion exposed the tracks. At right, the hikers work their way down the steep, deeply eroded slopes of a nearby canyon.

A cross a rippled sand dune, Death Valley creatures slither and crawl. When threatened, the circus beetle (above) stands on its head and kicks its legs in a bluff display, a maneuver that earned the insect its name. A sidewinder thrusts itself forward in S-shaped undulations, leaving an unmistakable trail. Two hornlike projections above the eyes distinguish this species of rattlesnake.

PRECEDING PAGES: Tawny dunes, shaped by shifting desert winds, smother a 14-square-mile area in the central part of the valley. Dune ridges shelter growths of saltbush, pickleweed, and inkweed.

by the time we pulled up at the Inyo mining camp. With the sun warm on our backs, we wandered through the site, past its rusting machinery and frame buildings of bleached and splintered wood. A mill which had processed the ore stood just a little apart from the kitchen, mess hall, and three small bunkhouses. There were no saloons and no gambling halls, nothing to suggest gunfights, poker games, and rowdy Saturday nights. The scene told of scant comfort, few conveniences, and hard work.

The opposite was true at Greenwater, a short-lived boomtown just outside the monument on the eastern slopes of the Black Mountains. There miners rushed to what promoters advertised as "the Greatest Copper Camp on Earth." But the hopeful, the gullible, and the drifters were left with little to do but nurse their futile dreams. Although the initial strike in 1905 yielded copper-rich ore, the vein went "neither up, down, nor sideways," wrote historian Harold O. Weight. Not a single one of the 2,500 recorded claims brought in anything worthwhile.

But the town, whose population grew to about a thousand, had several saloons, stores, a bank, a post office, and two newspapers, and it did produce its share of shoot-outs and shenanigans. Take Harold Weight's account of the funeral of Billy Robinson, "dead of the DT's after a prolonged binge. The saints, the sinners, and the in-betweens all attended Billy's rites, and Tiger Lil placed five aces in his hand, pressed close to his breast: 'So he'll look natural.' "

Copper drew people to Greenwater, and silver lured them to Panamint City; borax, lead, and gold brought others for a brief and hectic time to mining camps that are now ghost towns or have vanished completely. Places like Skidoo, Schwaub, Leadfield, Chloride City.

It was gold fever that impelled white men to Death Valley in the first place. Impatient to reach the goldfields of California, several groups of forty-niners broke off from a wagon train creaking south from Salt Lake City on a route that would make a long detour around the Sierra Nevada. In their haste, some forty-niners, including the Bennett and Arcane families, sought a shortcut going due west. They found instead, as they blundered into Death Valley in December 1849, months of hardship and despair.

After crossing a series of deserts and bleak hills in Nevada, and driving their weary, starving oxen and lumbering wagons up a rocky wash of the Funerals, the gold-seekers were stricken by the sight of the barren salt flats and snow-covered escarpment of the Panamints blocking their path.

Scholars dispute the precise routes the different bands of forty-niners took out of the valley, but LeRoy Johnson is convinced he has traced the Manly-Rogers trail. A superb outdoorsman and tireless hiker, he has dedicated much of his spare time since 1971 to tramping through the southern Panamints and the desert ranges between Death Valley and Los Angeles, trying to match the text of Manly's journal to the terrain.

While the disheartened Bennett and Arcane party camped beside a water hole in the valley, and waited with only stringy ox meat and preparations of ox blood, ox hide, and ox intestines to sustain them, William Lewis Manly and John Rogers set out in a desperate effort to find help and a way through the mountains.

At the head of Warm Spring Canyon, where LeRoy thinks Manly and Rogers camped their first night out, we were blasted by wind. LeRoy tied

Devils Golf Course: tortured legacy of a lake that dried up 2,000 years ago. The cracked lumps form when salty groundwater rises to the surface. The water evaporates, and the salt crystallizes, breaking the crust into bizarre patterns.

his hat more firmly under his chin; I burrowed deeper inside my parka; Paul wore a wool cap and gloves; even LeRoy's ebullient sons were subdued.

Manly and Rogers had no warm jackets, only half a blanket and one thin summer coat against the cold; rawhide moccasins to protect their feet from the rocks and snow; and a few spoonfuls of rice and tea and a knapsack of dried ox meat.

LeRoy set an easy pace up the steep slope to the snow-covered summit of what he calls Manly Lookout. On top, the land fell away, and before us to the west we saw another desert basin—the Panamint Valley—and more sere mountains—the Slate and Argus ranges—and still another desert and another range, and far to the north a great sweep of mountains shining with snow: the lofty Sierra Nevada. "This is where Manly and Rogers came to the stark realization that help was still a long way off," said LeRoy.

Ten days and some 200 miles later the two men staggered into a ranch north of the San Fernando Valley, where they bought supplies and then began the long, hard trek back.

We picked up the Manly-Rogers trail again when we explored Redlands Canyon, which LeRoy believes was the men's route back to the valley, and the way they led the families out. We followed LeRoy down the canyon, finding a beauty in the flood-polished walls. A sparrow chirped sweetly on a ledge above, and Paul answered with a song as sweet.

We came to a small precipice that LeRoy calls Ox-jump Fall. We scrambled down the dry fall, where he believes the pioneers lowered their children on ropes and pushed their enfeebled animals to a sprawling but safe landing on sand piled below.

The two smallest children were tucked into the pockets of saddlebags slung across the back of one of the oxen. The two older children rode astride. The adults walked. "The mothers," Manly wrote, "picked out soft places on which to place their poor blistered feet . . . and each foot was so badly affected that they did not know on which one to limp. But still they moved. . . ."

For the bedraggled caravan of Bennetts and Arcanes, the scenery was nothing to admire; it was a wash to walk, a ridge to climb, a torment to endure. For them it was a godforsaken land, and they named it Death Valley.

S tories of the ordeals of the forty-niners did not deter the restless, hardy men who tramped through every canyon and side canyon prospecting for silver and gold. "It's incredible where you find some of the prospect holes they dug," said LeRoy, pointing to a scar in the heights of Surprise Canyon.

We had driven outside the monument along the west side of the Panamints to the mouth of Surprise Canyon, and Paul was piloting his van up a tortuous trail that twisted alongside a stream. He turned the steering wheel continually, left to right and back again. We couldn't tell when we left the rocky, chaotic trail: The jolts and lurches were all the same.

Finally, jarred but intact, we arrived at the once-notorious Panamint City, nine miles uphill and 7,500 feet high. Back in the 1870's, outlaws found that the gorge of Surprise Canyon made a perfect hideout, and they could also do a little prospecting while there. A silver strike in 1873 produced a boisterous, wide-open boomtown that had a reputation for violence rivaling the most lawless places of the West. In three years, 57 people were buried in the cemetery at Sour Dough Canyon, most of them dead of "lead poisoning." Wells Fargo refused to transport the silver, but mine owners knew how to outwit bandits. They cast the silver into 450-pound balls—too heavy for horsemen to make off with—and blithely hauled them out in open wagons. Of the old town only a few walls and the

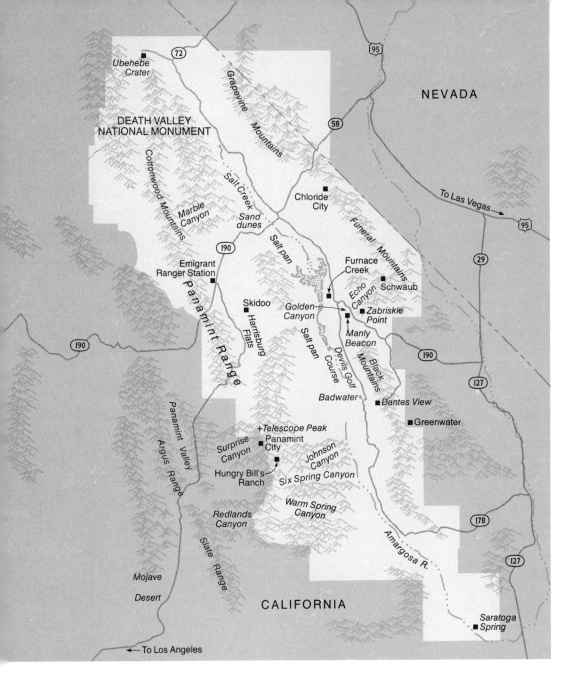

Mountains edge Death Valley National Monument—3,000 square miles of sand, rocks, and sunbaked canyons. The monument, established in 1933, ranges from mountains studded with bristlecone pines to a barren salt pan on the basin floor. Its only river, the Amargosa, remains a dry wash most of the year.

tall smokestack of the smelter remain. The silver boom was ending when a flood in 1876 swept away the town and the road.

We spent the night in a shack built by miners who had tried their luck in more recent times. With a fire muttering in the potbellied stove and candlelight to mellow the darkness, we dubbed our shelter the Plywood Palace. And it was a room with a view. In the early morning, I looked out the window upon a high slope wooded with junipers and piñons, their thin ranks growing more dense in gulches still choked with snow. Above, the ridges—white at the skyline—borrowed the colors of a fiery sunrise.

Somehow I had assumed that the time of the solitary prospector had passed. But halfway down Surprise Canyon we discovered he's alive and doing well. Rangy, six feet six inches tall, George Novak squints at you from the shade of a weathered gray fedora. Only the white stubble on his cheeks and chin hints at his 58 years.

Lighting the bent stub of his cigarette for a second time, he told us that up until now he's been locating likely veins in these hills; the mining will come later. An assortment of ore samples crowded a bookcase outside his trailer. Tiny cups filled with acid covered a table. "I do my own chemical work, testing the ores myself so I know what I've got. I've been banging around this country for 40 years, but this time I've found the mother lode. I hit a new strike that sure looks good—32 ounces of silver a ton.

"So far it's been all put out and no take in," he said, spitting once before he tried lighting the cigarette stub again.

George introduced us to his son, Rocky, who goes off once in a while to work in a factory, and brings in enough money to keep his dad going.

"I've had lots of partners that just never panned out, so I decided to raise me one. Might as well name him Rocky if he's going to stomp around these rocks all day."

"Do you ever get lonely?" I asked.

"I'm so doggone busy thinking about what I'm doing, I don't have time. Oh, you catch yourself talking to yourself. Sometimes I lose track of the days. I mark 'em off on a calendar, and then I wonder if I forgot. So I cross a day off again. Pretty soon I find myself a week ahead."

George doesn't dream of prosperity. "I'm not going to go into big production. If I can knock down four ton a day, I'll be happy. I can make enough at that to stay independent.

"Mining's a good life."

There were many more prospectors in the backcountry in the late forties when Russ Johnson was packing supplies and equipment to a gold mine in the Cottonwood Mountains, in the northern Panamints. "I'd collect rocks going up the washes, and the old prospectors could nearly always tell where each piece came from. But those men weren't interested in mining. When they located a prospect, they'd just sell it to the first taker and set off into the desert again, dreaming of a bigger bonanza," said Russ, a broad-shouldered, easygoing man from Minnesota; he left home 45 years ago to find someplace warm to live.

It would take Russ five hours to lead his string of mules from Emigrant Ranger Station up into the high basins of the Cottonwoods, where shaggy Joshua trees grope skyward with bristling clusters of stiff, dagger-shaped leaves. "Sometimes during a long trip, I'd get a little skittish and take a shortcut," Russ reminisced. "I remember once I started down a draw I'd never been in before. Halfway, I came to a dry fall I wasn't so sure I could handle. But I knew I couldn't get back up the last one I'd slid down. That's when I started to wonder whether I'd made a mistake. I left the horses and mules loose up at the top and started skidding down. Before I got a third of the way, the horses were sliding behind me, sparks flying from their shoes. I zigzagged from side to side, trying to keep out of their way. And then came the mules."

Russ smiled when I told him I found it hard to visualize the animals sliding down the slope. "The stock raised around here can handle these rock piles. They tuck their rumps under them and bring their front legs forward. They slide with their hind legs and walk with their front. But it seems to me they always wait for you to go down first."

Later, Paul and I headed for the Cottonwoods, too, to hike up Marble Canyon with Pete Sanchez, a dynamo of a park ranger and the natural resource manager for the monument. "I'm the guy that fights to preserve the plants and animals native to this desert," he said. This puts Pete squarely against the hardy tamarisk, a Mediterranean tree that was introduced into California as a windbreak. It competes for water so successfully with local plants that it can take over. Pete has spearheaded a Park Service program to eliminate these trees.

But it's the subject of burros that brings a look of exasperation to his dark, piercing eyes. "We've got an overpopulation of burros—animals which don't belong here in the first place—and they're overgrazing and trampling the vegetation in large areas of the monument.

"It's not just that it looks bad, or is unnatural. There is a grave danger that native plants and animals may be snuffed out. For example, every time we take a census of the desert bighorn sheep we find that its numbers are going down. More roads, more people in the backcountry, and the drying up of springs all may be contributing to the declining population, now down to about 500 sheep. But after all, the burro is competing with the bighorn in the desert, which has a limited capacity to support life."

Scowling clouds were gathering as we passed the region of the sand dunes. The wind ripples and drifts looked less remarkable in the flat, noonday light than at sunrise and sunset. By the time we neared Marble Canyon, roiling clouds spanned the sky and swirled down to the horizon in a soft white mist. The Cottonwoods loomed dark and sullen where clouds descended in columns of rain. To the east, shafts of sunlight and patches of shadow patterned the rose and red colors of the Grapevine Mountains.

Suddenly a murky, yellow dust squall appeared on the northern edge of the valley. In seconds it spiraled upward to perhaps 3,000 feet. One, two, three more squalls appeared in unbelievably swift succession, churned upward, coalesced, and advanced down the valley as a curtain of darkness. We retreated to the car, buffeted by the wind but safe inside, while the sand blasted the windshield and the finish. Then, as suddenly as it had begun, the siege was over. The fog of dust veered to the southeast, and a crescent of blue sky emerged above the Cottonwoods.

"The dangerous thing about hiking in a canyon during a rainstorm is that you can't see out," said Pete, as we shouldered our packs. "Even if there's just a little shower overhead, you can't be sure it's not raining hard two miles up a side canyon. But if I thought conditions were right for a flash flood, I wouldn't be here."

And Pete is a man you can trust. Also, if you can keep up with him, he turns a hike into a series of fascinating discoveries. My eyes might have passed over the time-dimmed Indian petroglyphs—lines, circles, animal profiles. I would have overlooked the gravel high up on the ledges, evidence of flood levels in times past. I might not have noticed the desert varnish, a satiny brown patina of manganese and iron oxides that covers exposed rock surfaces in hot, arid lands. Or the tracks of a deer. Or the desert pavement, where sandblasted pebbles form a mosaic.

As we entered the narrows of Marble Canyon, the sky shrank to a sliver of blue directly overhead. Sheer limestone walls loomed above us, confining us in a shadowy world of deep stillness. It seemed I could hear the roar of raging rivers and the boom of ricocheting boulders, for the scoured and battered walls of the canyon and the dry meanders twisting through it speak with a clear and eloquent voice.

As we progressed up the canyon and back down the following day, every detail of the landscape drew Pete's enthusiasm and erudition—the falcon flying overhead, the harvester ants carrying seeds to their underground nests, the bats swooping past us in the dusk. Pete led us to a wide patch of rough gray rock that looked like lumpy plaster on the smooth face of the limestone. "A fine example of fault breccia," he said. He explained that we were looking at rock that had been crushed and ground between two limestone blocks slipping and rubbing against each other. We could see the debris, consolidated now into a conglomerate-like rock called breccia, only where water had eroded one side of the limestone.

While earthquakes shook the region, and mountain ranges rose, a long block of earth slipped, dropping deeper and deeper, forming a valley without the aid of a river. Geologists call such a depression a structural valley, and in Death Valley it is 4 to 16 miles wide and 150 miles long.

Long after the valley formed, the climate turned cooler and wetter. Meltwater from glaciers in the Sierra Nevada to the west, along with increased precipitation, collected in a series of lakes that filled and overflowed into successively lower desert basins. In Death Valley, Lake Manly formed. Then the climate changed, and the waters grew warmer and saltier as the lakes slowly dried up. The fishes died out, one after the other, but the desert pupfish hung on, surviving in deep water holes, isolated springs, and in Salt Creek, a sluggish, tiny stream just a few inches deep.

I complained to Pete that I had prowled the boardwalk the Park Service had built along the creek, but I had seen no pupfish. "In winter they bury themselves in the mud at the bottom. By March, thousands of them will be schooling and scooting up and down the creek," he explained.

Then he plunged into a discourse on the breeding behavior of the hardy creature, no bigger than a child's finger, that has adapted to life in water at least twice as salty as the ocean. During the height of the breeding season in April, the male turns an iridescent blue, and stakes out his territory along the bank. He cruises the boundaries, chasing other males out, until a stronger or bigger male comes along. When a female comes by, he'll sidle up to her, and the two swim off together.

Unlike the pupfish, some animals—the mastodon, the camel, a species of large cat—did not survive environmental changes. On another excursion Paul and I hiked the far reaches of one of the canyons to see the tracks of these animals still preserved in a hillside of shale.

In the days that followed, we journeyed to the region of the half-mile-wide Ubehebe Crater in the north, where the land lies black beneath a blanket of volcanic ash, and we strolled beside the surge of greenery flourishing on the edges of Saratoga Spring far to the south. We walked across the depths of the salt pan where ridges and pinnacles of salt glitter like jewels in an unearthly emptiness, and at the same time gazed at the wintry splendor of snow-mantled peaks. Everywhere we went, up and down the valley's great length, the landscape was amazingly varied and endlessly beautiful.

I missed the spectacle of springtime in a wet year, when winter showers bring forth a paradise of wild flowers. The fall of rain for the season was too meager to stir the seeds lying beneath the parched earth. But there was beauty in the colors of the contorted, water-hewn rock, and in the drama of changing light and shifting shadows. And—in a valley named for death—there is a special beauty in the triumph of life over the desert's awesome heat and drought.

Steep limestone wall, seamed in shades of blue, provides precarious footholds for Park Ranger Pete Sanchez and the author in Marble Canyon. Floodwaters churning with sand and gravel have slowly ground the wall smooth.

In the harsh badlands of Golden Canyon (right), a family strides past a weathered rock face. On a flank of Manly Beacon (left), they follow a trail that winds through a maze of bare clay hills. They heed a Park Service injunction and carry "plenty of water," for thirsts build quickly in the hot dry air of March. Above, the immense slope of the peak dwarfs the family. This welter of hills, once a lake bed, grew when forces within the earth lifted and folded layers of sediment, and countless rains scoured canyons.

Crowned by sprays of blossoms (right), brittlebushes survive year round; a brown-eyed evening primrose (below, left) and a sand verbena sprout and flower only in response to rains. A side-blotched lizard warms itself on a cool day by absorbing heat from a rock, as well as the sun.

PRECEDING PAGES: Glorious profusion of golden evening primroses carpets the desert after a winter of timely and adequate rainfall.

Lake Clark

The Essence of Alaska: Tundra, Glaciers, Mountains

By John Kauffmann
Photographs by Jim Brandenburg

Think of all the splendors that bespeak Alaska: glaciers, volcanoes, alpine spires, wild rivers, lakes with grayling on the rise. Picture coasts feathered with countless seabirds. Imagine dense forests and far-sweeping tundra, herds of caribou, great roving bears. Now concentrate all these and more into less than one percent of the state—and behold the Lake Clark region, Alaska's epitome. It is not the state's biggest, highest, or most remote wilderness. But it *is* one of the most varied, boasting almost every type of Alaskan landscape.

Surprisingly few people know the Lake Clark area well, though it is only an hour by small plane from Anchorage, where nearly half of all Alaskans live. Most of these city dwellers have never visited the mountains they see glimmering on their western horizon, mountains that only recently have been included in a new 2.5-million-acre unit of our National Park System: the Lake Clark National Monument.

The preserve lies just west of Cook Inlet. *Stormbird*, a 65-foot former Army boat, refitted and skippered by charter captain Clem Tillion, took me there through the inlet's choppy swells. With us were Paul Fritz, park planner for the national monument, and several Native Alaskans, village representatives who were looking over their lands for potential settlement sites. Near the monument's southeastern corner, at magnificent Tuxedni Bay, two gateposts tower nearly two miles high. Backlighted and pale with snow, they seem at first immutably frozen, yet steam seeps from the side of one. They are active volcanoes: Iliamna and Redoubt.

Other, lesser mountain steeps join them, walling off the Tuxedni coast with an awesome fortress that grew steadily more imposing during our sea-level approach. White cataracts spumed down furrowed cliffs hundreds of feet high.

"This is the beginning of the country I really like," Clem said. "It's

River genesis: Silver meltwaters from a glacier's tip wander down a valley in Alaska's Lake Clark National Monument. It and many other glacial streams course this newly designated wilderness preserve southwest of Anchorage.

clear and clean and absolutely wild. Like looking at the world as it used to be." Before us, beluga whales sounded in the icy waters of Tuxedni Bay. Double-crested cormorants wheeled above the high rock prow of Chisik Island, refuge for tens of thousands of seabirds. Sea life of 150 million years ago—ammonites and mussels now preserved in stone—showed in the crumbling, layered cliffs of Fossil Point.

As in the Arctic, summers here are prolific and short, though not as brief as farther north. Tuxedni Bay's sloping ramparts come to life while you watch, growing so alder-green that, through narrowed eyes forgetful of latitude, they seem to form an almost Caribbean coast.

To the north, glaciers spread their outwash across a coastal plain patterned by grassy glades and forest clumps. Great braided rivers, heavy with silt, dump endless streams of what looks like liquid concrete into Cook Inlet's surging tides.

Following the coast southwestward, we came to long beaches and gentle forestlands. At Glacier Spit we met Bob and Mary Haeg, former general contractors who, in 1975, made their home beneath sheltering cottonwoods of Chinitna Bay. Out in the barnyard, above the quacking and honking of ducks and geese, their 13-year-old son, David, introduced me to Tasha the mare, Custer the goat, and Sheba the family dog. Sheba "runs bears out of the yard 'cause she's the boss."

"We've had no trouble with the bears, really," Mary assured me. "We like them alive. One spends a lot of time down there in that cottonwood grove, but we just honk the horn of our pickup when we go down to the beach, to let him know we're coming."

Backcountry living has its hardships, of course. All supplies, from toothpaste to motor oil, must be flown or boated in. David "goes to school" by correspondence course, "but is doing better than he could in the city," Mary told me.

"We're where we want to be," said Bob. "All our lives we've loved wilderness. Even in Minnesota we had a cabin. We knew then that nobody truly lives off the land anymore—that's for dreamers. But we also knew that if we could make just a little money, we could have a good life."

Each summer, the Haegs earn that cash by netting and selling salmon. Winters? "Well, we do whatever we feel like doing," Bob said, "learn ham radio, work on our nets, watch the otters, the seals, the eagles, the ptarmigan coming down from high country."

Throughout the monument, "high country" is never very far away. Iliamna and Redoubt are but two peaks in the jagged Chigmit Mountains bordering Cook Inlet. The National Park Service has termed the mountains here "a frenzy of peaks." The Chigmits form the meeting place of the massive Alaska and Aleutian ranges that dominate the state's southern half, and it is as if colliding mountain waves have thrown up a storm of rock. To some, they are Alaska's Alps, so tight and deep a mountain maze that each portion is a private world. Only the doughtiest trekkers have crossed the Chigmits on foot, braving flood and thicket and crevasse. Most visitors to Lake Clark charter a plane or take a more roundabout route by scheduled air service out of Anchorage.

Fly west through Merrill Pass—a major cleft in the Chigmit chain— and you crane from window to window. Glaciers pour down every few miles. Crags soar into the clouds above. Now they resemble cathedral spires, now gnashing sharks' teeth, crowded row upon row. A particularly spectacular pinnacle has earned the title, The Tusk.

It is one of few geographic names in this backcountry, a fact that makes the region all the more alluring to me. Naming must have seemed

*Wild Alaska in miniature, the 2.5-million-acre Lake Clark National Monument
offers a sampling of many of the state's wilderness delights—in less than one percent*

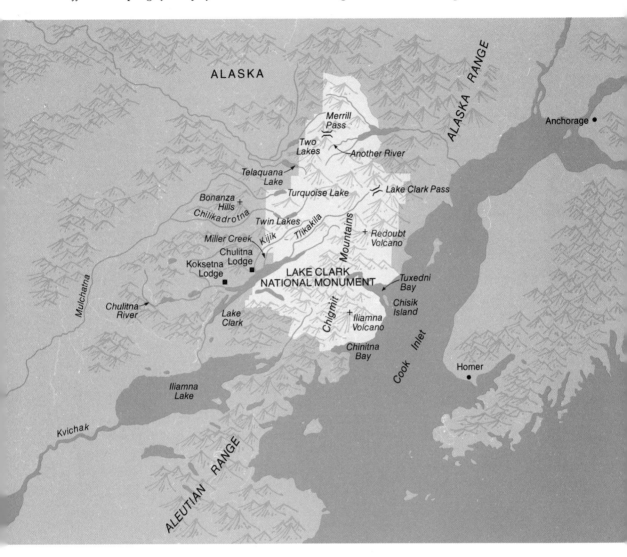

*of the space. Marshy seacoasts rise to meet the Chigmit Mountains, which curtain
off interior highlands dappled with lakes, tundra, and forests. There waterways
teem with salmon, trout, and grayling; moose, bear, Dall sheep, and caribou roam
the wide-open hinterlands.*

all but hopeless to the surveyors of the early 1900's who toiled in with
packhorses. Dragging through the alder thickets and boulder fields as little
as a mile a day, they came to still another torrent, draining yet another
pass. And this one they named. They called it Another River.

One senses the feat of penetrating Chigmit country from old government reports: "The streams that drain it are unnavigable torrents. . . .
many portions of the region are so rugged, so lofty, and so filled with active
glaciers that they can be reached only by severe alpine climbing, or not at
all." In 1975 a Park Service study team hiked the area and failed to be spotted from the air at its rendezvous point, even though it had spread out "a
half acre of orange tents, tarps, and silver space blankets and had
a smoky fire going. This . . . shows the unlikelihood of a party in trouble

getting aid in time to be of real use." I recount this to make clear that the Chigmits are not for the novice, the casual, the ill-prepared. Glaciers chink the passes; alders choke the valleys. The Chigmits represent mountain wilderness at its very finest.

Their westward slopes are clothed alternately with low tundra vegetation, willow thicket, and forest. North of Lake Clark, glacial valleys hold handsome lakes—Twin, Turquoise, Telaquana, Two Lakes, and others— set gleaming at the edge of the mountains like pendant jewels. Their outlet rivers course across lowlands toward far blue hills. Here the Chilikadrotna and Mulchatna rivers, like the Tlikakila farther east, have been recommended for inclusion in the National Wild and Scenic Rivers System. They drain southwesterly, ultimately into great Bristol Bay, site of the world's largest sockeye salmon fishery. Prominent in the region is the 50-mile-long finger of water that lends its name to the monument.

It's hard to describe lakes—their moods change so quickly, now pale green in sunlight, now burnished pewter after clouds close down. Geologists who first scouted Lake Clark departed from matter-of-fact reporting to call it "a magnificent body of water." Bush pilot Hank Rust, who has flown this country for nearly 20 years, uses less formal eloquence: "Summer or winter, there isn't a prettier place in the world."

I had a chance to test Hank's pronouncement when he flew me to Lake Clark in early March. As Merrill Pass gives access westward, so Lake Clark Pass slices southwestward through equally spectacular country to the lake itself, and to the Iliamna region beyond. The pass was a dream world of white snow speckled with spruces in the valley bottoms. On both sides, ice fields lay atop the ranges like dozing polar bears with glacier paws extending down the canyonsides. Pillars of blue ice masked summer's waterfalls. Far below, moose ranged a frozen slough; a lone wolverine loped across the frozen surface of the Tlikakila River.

With us was the 25-year-old caretaker of Hank's commodious Chulitna Lodge, Bob Tracey, who six years before had followed the mountains north to Alaska to trap and to help guides like Hank. The shining surface of Lake Clark was green marble, its bare surface veined with white where snow filled long cracks in the ice.

A chorus of joyous yelps and howls greeted us as we landed and walked ashore. Bob's seven sled dogs were eager for a run. Puddles, his lead dog, stood up for a hug. Stoney wagged a big hello. Bob greeted them all, Joey and Polly, Chun-Tum, Tiger, and Pup. Soon they were harnessed for a check run of Bob's trapline. "Jump in," said Bob, as the huskies strained against the tie rope. He released it and we shot forward as from a rocket launcher. Even though securely seated in the nine-foot freighter sled, I hung on for dear life as it bucked and plunged down the narrow, icy trail. The dogs' first brief burst of speed had us traveling at more than 15 miles an hour. Then they settled down to a steady rush, and we slammed down into a gully, then up and out, sluing around bends, ricocheting off logs and bushes, but always speeding surely ahead. Seven powerful furry bodies were running whatever the musher's equivalent is for "hell-for-leather." How Bob, riding the runners right behind me, ever stayed on I cannot imagine, but he steered us through every tight turn, avoiding now a tree, now a sharp snag, until the dogs were flying across the open spaces flanking the Kijik River. "There's an old saying that the hardest-working dog is the guy behind the sled," Bob quipped.

We halted now and then so Bob could check his traps, which some years stretch nearly 60 miles, around behind the mountains and down the lakeshore. At each stop I trod hard on the big iron claw that digs into the snow to brake the sled, nervously wondering if the dogs might tire of their routine and bolt for home. But every time, they rolled contentedly in the snow until Bob returned. At his command their start was so explosive that one time the sled tipped over and left me sprawled in the snow. Somehow Bob stayed with the sled. A quick grab and shout put him back in control, saving us a long walk home, and soon we were flying along the trail again.

"Want to go home, Tiger?" Bob called. "Gee! Puddles, gee!" "Henh! Henh!" he urged, whistling encouragement.

Few bush people want to put up with the work of maintaining dog teams, now that snowmobiles are available. Bob spends more than a month catching and drying salmon—thousands of them—just to feed his team. But dogs can go where snowmobiles founder, or break down, or run out of gas; and there's a joy in mushing that is bringing more and more Alaskans back to dog power.

Bob is one of the thirty or so wilderness addicts who have forsaken city amenities for Lake Clark's year-round charms. Their cabins nestle on the lakeshore here and there, among them one built years ago by Jay Hammond, Alaska's governor.

"I like that country as well as any place in the state," the governor told me in his Juneau office. "It's a microcosm of virtually all of the things Alaska is renowned for. I first saw Lake Clark when I was flying in on a hunting trip in 1947; I put up a tent at the upper end of the lake. Then an old settler told me about Miller Creek, where there is a stream and a good place for a garden. He had gone to Lake Clark as a young man. 'It's the most beautiful spot in the world, and I'm going to stay,' he had said, and he did—married a local girl and didn't get over to Anchorage for 30 years.

"As a veteran, I was able to homestead the land he had recommended," the governor continued, "and I've been working on the place ever since." Governor Hammond still gets there four or five times a year. "It's a good place to get away to," he mused, as his office door opened to let in more urgent state business.

At Koksetna Camp, on the shore of Lake Clark, Chuck and Sara Hornberger care for hunters, fishermen, and those who simply want the delicious combination of Lake Clark's mountainous panorama and Sara's homemade sourdough chocolate cake. Their greenhouse was bursting and the garden was lush with vegetables and ripening berries when I was there in the summer. The steady "thunk-thunk-thunk" of an ax revealed where their daughter, Linda, was peeling logs to build her own cabin.

Surrounded by wilderness, the Hornbergers are studies in self-reliance. Chuck is the resident carpenter, electrician, mechanic, welder, pilot, and general roustabout. Sara manages the domestic chores, garden, and greenhouse, and keeps the region's most extensive lending library—featuring everything from Sir Walter Scott to John Irving. Linda bakes brownies and fells trees with equal ease.

Their life-style is rustic, but by no means primitive. Koksetna includes half a dozen buildings, all designed and built by Chuck. In addition to the main house, there are two guest cabins, a storage barn, bath and laundry house, workshop, and more. The workshop is especially well stocked, for Chuck maintains two planes, two snowmobiles, several boats, a tractor, and a backhoe—all without benefit of a corner hardware store.

A bank of storage batteries, periodically recharged by a windmill, powers the lights, electric tools, and citizens-band radio. Wood stoves—wrought from gasoline drums—ensure comfort through the winter.

Whatever the Hornbergers cannot grow or make on the spot is flown in from Anchorage, usually in case lots. Water is hauled from the lake all year. Vegetables must be planted, harvested, and put up for winter. In return for all their toil, Sara and Chuck and Linda enjoy a near-total freedom. "There's lots to do, but you do it when it seems best," Chuck grinned from under his knitted watch cap, jammed down to his eyebrows in front and cocked up in back, Navy-style. He admitted that visitors often envy his independence.

"They'll say things like, 'You're a bum! You don't go to work every day; what do you do?' "

Sara answered, "I don't have enough hours in the day to do all I have to get done, the writing, sewing, gardening." A former teacher and school administrator, she now presides over a school board responsible for a district 450 miles long. Like her husband, she loves the bush too much to trade it for an easier, citified life.

Chuck explained: "Once you get to know the country and feel what it's like to be 'unwound,' you realize what a place like this means."

To illustrate, he gave me a morning's boat trip up the Chulitna River, which edges the lodge site. Moose splashed off through the marshes; pike after voracious pike struck at the streamer fly I cast into likely sloughs. The Chulitna is not a salmon river, but the fish flourish in other waters around Lake Clark. During the summer spawning season, they crowd rivers and lakes in vast schools.

On an island at the head of Lake Clark, the newly completed Van Valin Island Lodge commands the Tlikakila's gorge, a scene where "the northern lights are right *there*." So Sharon Van Valin told me, adding, "I have to stay away from that window or I'd never get any work done." She and her husband, Glen, both teachers, came to Alaska in 1964. "At first I felt that I couldn't like it in bush Alaska, but decided it was worth one school-year's try," said Sharon. "By Christmas I knew I never wanted to leave." They had flown over the island on their way to their teaching jobs, later applied to settle on a parcel of government land there, and built a cabin for summers, all the while planning for the time they could "help people appreciate this area."

Assisting Glen with the lodge construction when I first visited the island was Jack Ross, who also lives on the lake. Unlike some Alaskans, both Glen and Jack welcome protection for the Lake Clark area, though it will mean curtailment of developments, at least on the public lands.

"I want something left for my grandchildren," Jack explained. "Without protection even this big area would be used up eventually. Someday they'd mow down the trees like they're doing elsewhere. I can't understand why people don't believe they have to take care. All they have to do is look behind them to see the mistakes."

Numerous rivers course the rolling foothills and high plains north and west of Lake Clark. Much of this region is alpine tundra: spongy in summer, pond-spangled, vast as the eye can see. Empty? Not so. In summer it teems with life, but life spread out across its fragile surface. Tundra can be boggy in the valleys, and is almost always tussocky and mosquito-ridden, a nightmare for hikers. But atop Lake Clark's foothills the tundra is dry, and offers fine walking. Here, too, are the predominantly spruce woodlands known as taiga, where the soothing, astringent aroma of Labrador tea plants wafts through the air. I longed to experience this country firsthand.

"Come with us," invited Sierra Club trip leader Blaine LeCheminant and Alaskan wilderness guide Bob Waldrop.

For two weeks, their backpacking group would be out of touch with civilization, hiking the taiga and tundra from Portage Lake, across the Kijik River, over a pass to Twin Lakes, and (Continued on page 201)

"Why me?" a plump coho salmon seems to implore in a snout-to-nose confrontation with Crey Weston, a commercial fisherman working near the monument's southeastern shore.

*W*atery arena of Cook Inlet surges with varied marine and coastal wildlife along the monument's edge. A 15-foot beluga whale swims toward the foamy wake left by another as it sounded (below). The whales cruise the rich, muddy shallows of Tuxedni Bay for salmon, herring, or shrimp. Several hundred white-skinned belugas patrol these waters in summer, and some stay year round. Cliff-dwelling kittiwakes (left and bottom left) wheel and dive off Chisik Island, a national wildlife refuge and important nesting site for thousands of seabirds. Above Chinitna Bay, another arm of Cook Inlet, a tufted puffin, or sea parrot (middle left), takes home a beakful of fingerlings; its abrasive tongue and massive bill enable the bird to catch and carry as many as ten small fish at a time.

FOLLOWING PAGES: *Inland from the coast, lake-spangled stretches of muskeg and spruce forest alternate with slopes of low-growing alders. A snowcapped but still-active volcano—10,197-foot Redoubt—dominates the horizon.*

*H*omeward-bound traffic navigates the preserve's lakes and streams each summer as sockeye salmon leave the Pacific Ocean and turn brilliant red as they forge upstream to their ancestral spawning grounds (right). Egg-laden females clear shallow nests in river gravel while males spar for nuptial privilege (left). The hook-snouted winner—its jaws so deformed by physiological changes during the

spawning season that it cannot close its mouth—approaches the female (above). The fish mate by depositing eggs and milt simultaneously. The female then moves upstream, digs additional nests, and mates with the same or a different male until she exhausts her supply of three to four thousand eggs. Death soon comes to both adults. Their orphaned offspring hatch months later and spend a year or two in fresh water before heading seaward. After two to three years of ocean life, the salmon mature and return to breed and die. Of the many salmon tributaries within the monument, most drain to the southwest into Bristol Bay, a magnet for as many as 53 million sockeyes in good years, and the site of the world's largest sockeye fishery.

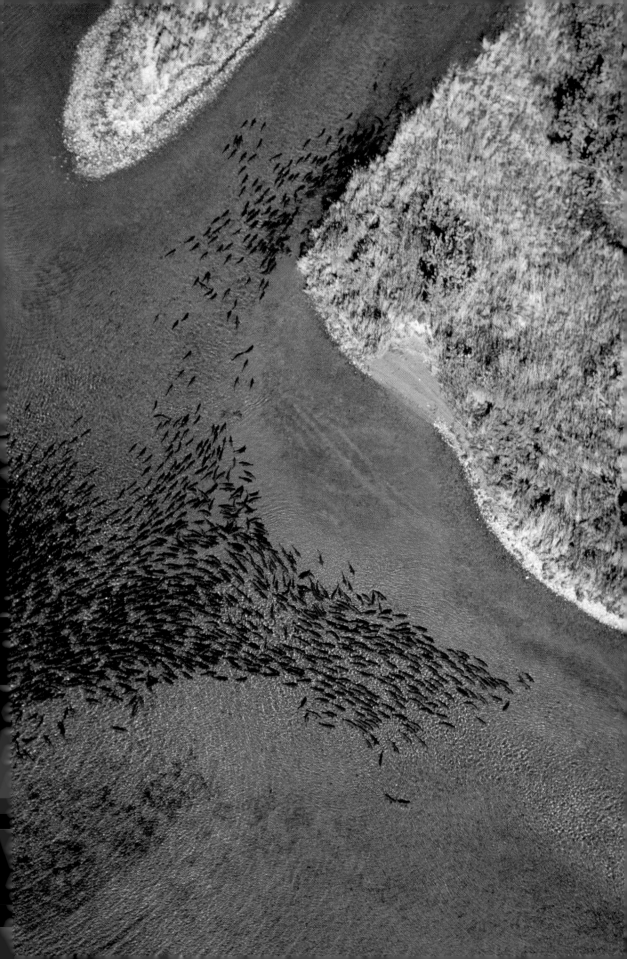

*E*arly-morning mists ribbon spruce forests and sun-burnished summits bordering
Lake Clark, a 50-mile-long finger of water that gave the monument its name.
"Summer or winter, there isn't a prettier place in the world," says bush pilot
Hank Rust. The lake's forested shores provide ample forage for porcupines.

FOLLOWING PAGES:
*Statuesque Dall sheep peers
shoreward from an unnamed
island in Lake Clark.*

193

*A*utumn *blush of alpine bearberry leaves brightens this tundra, a stark land above timberline. The leaves turn crimson (left) as winter approaches, and crowd pale "antlers" of reindeer moss, actually a lichen. Sedges, grasses, and other tiny but tenacious plants complete the tundra spectrum, proliferating where no trees take root. Though low-growing and easily scarred by man, such living mats retain water that might otherwise erode the thin tundra soil and flood valleys below. The plants provide food for roving caribou (right), and arctic ground squirrels, ptarmigan, hares, and other herbivores. They, in turn, support populations of red fox (opposite), a hunter equally at home in tundra or forest.*

Hewn from the Alaskan wilderness, a backcountry homestead hugs the shore of Lake Clark. Since 1974, the Hornberger family has lived permanently at the lake, in a complex of buildings they designed and built. At left, Linda Hornberger notches logs that will become the walls of her new cabin. Earmuffs (below) soften the chain saw's scream as she and her father, Chuck, ensure a close fit by "three-siding" a spruce log.
The greenhouse in the foreground and the derrick-like wind generator (opposite) permit this bush family two backcountry luxuries—electricity and fresh vegetables.

on to Turquoise Lake, where a plane would meet them. The hikers came from ten states and a dozen vocations, and ranged in age from mid-20's to 50's. Blaine, a California schoolteacher, was returning to Alaska for more memories—what he called "inner images to cherish in the mind." A young librarian from Milwaukee had opened a special bank account to save for this trip, her first to Alaska.

One of the women confided, "I've never been where you couldn't get out when you wanted to." Her remark reminded me how different Alaska is from most other wild areas in our nation, where if need be one can always make it back to civilization in a day or two. In contrast, we were scores of miles from a road—any road.

Bob, lanky veteran of many Alaskan treks and a professional guide for 15 years, was as excited as any of us by the trip's prospects. "This is not just the State of Alaska," he exulted. "This is the state of euphoria!"

"Look," he exclaimed, as we set out from mountain-girded Portage Lake, "that view could be of the Brooks Range, and, over there, a scene out of Mount McKinley park. Something of most parts of Alaska is represented here, but more tersely. The Brooks Range and other Alaskan wilderness areas are elaborate novels; this is a poem."

The wildlife helped us through some tough thickets. Although the shy animals kept to their secluded haunts, the paths they had worn were a boon. Pity the poor backpacker without his four-legged trailblazers, I thought, as we struggled along under 60-pound packs.

As we hiked, summer flowers brightened the way—fireweed, lupine, cinquefoil. In autumn we would have seen tundra vegetation that had the rich colors of an Oriental rug. I was grateful that we were not hiking in the formidable wilderness nearer Cook Inlet: There the steep backcountry carries a double curse of alder and devils club. The first grows in wiry tangles that never miss a chance to batter shin or ankle; the second has prickles that can cause painful lacerations.

Bob Waldrop keeps a journal of the trips he guides, and in it I had read of another group's hike in that more rugged area of the monument. In a couple of ways, their experiences previewed our own. From their trip:

"By the day's end, I was wet to the skin over 100% of my body. Not a dry thread. Quicksand, cliffs, devils club, raw legs from alders & D.C. [devils club], bruised shins, glacial river dunkings, & ooze to my waist are some of the sensations of an agonizing day. Amazingly, the group's spirits are high. . . ."

Several days later, they had to ford a foaming rapid. The freezing waters raced by, rolling boulders and branches past them. Bob, armed only with a walking stick, staggered through the liquid ice and tied a rope to the far bank. The plan was to cross singly, using the knotted rope as a handrail. The method worked well until one of the smaller hikers began making her way through the torrent. Again, from Bob's journal: "Half way, after a good bit of head shaking & other signs of giving up to the river & cold, she slipped & fought well for hanging onto the rope but it slid thru her hands. . . . She swept, bobbing downstream, hands working to undo the pack, as I raced thru the rapid—totally unaware of the footing, cold, or force of the water—& I caught up to her 100' downstream, grabbing her

Summer bounty brings a proud smile to Sara Hornberger amid a rainbow of nasturtiums, snapdragons, dahlias, and other flowers grown "just for fun." The greenhouse, glassed with windows from an old salmon cannery and warmed by a homemade wood-burning stove, enables her to stretch Lake Clark's short growing season and produce a rich variety of fresh vegetables.

pack as she swept by. We were both glad to be there. I helped her out of the pack, pulled her ashore, onshore, gave her a hug. . . ."

I thought of her later, when our group came to a similar roaring torrent—the Kijik. How balefully cold it looked, raging down from glacial sources. Each rapid seemed to snarl with white teeth eager to attack bare legs. For an hour we wandered along bluffs and bars looking vainly for shallows somewhere amid the solid rush of opaque green river. Bob ranged ahead and returned at last wet but smiling, having found and tested a crossing. With three main channels to wade, we formed up into teams of four, held hands for mutual support, and edged in parallel to the current's thrust. It charged numbingly at knees and thighs, until our feet seemed about to float off the rocky bottom. We gripped each other in desperation, terrified that our balance would fail. We were faltering when Bob's long arm reached out to steady us ashore. A fire and hot drinks warmed feet and raised spirits.

From the Kijik, we climbed the pass leading to Twin Lakes, where we looked down on the two huge drops of blue pressed out of the white snow. Here we saw Dall sheep, a ewe and her lamb, climb effortlessly up a rock face that, to us, seemed vertical. They are almost ethereal beings, these pure white northern cousins of the bighorn, perfectly matched to their sheer surroundings. Seen wandering across a valley, they seem strangely out of place, like mountaineers on city streets.

Alaska can be a wilderness of rocks, a brutal tangle of alder and willow—and we had experienced both. But it also offers natural gardens of exquisite beauty: lichen beds, moss cushions, blueberry edgings heavily laden, amid graceful groves of spruce. Through such we walked toward the thoroughfare between the Twin Lakes.

We camped there one night in a quickening wind. While our group's anglers struck off in hopes of a trout-and-grayling supper, I wandered in vague exploration, meeting an arctic ground squirrel carrying a luscious-looking mushroom half as big as he was. This is *my* mushroom, he seemed to say, eyeing me coolly.

Next day we climbed again, up and down a mountain just for fun. "I feel so big, as if I fitted the country," shouted a Maryland housewife, standing atop a rock pinnacle with arms stretched wide. On another day, far below us in the valley of the Chilikadrotna River, small herds of caribou grazed. Several hundred more, ranked on a high tundra dome above us, watched us warily. They seemed a medieval army arrayed for battle, big-antlered bulls at front and center like a guard of crested knights.

Such herds of the north are among our continent's last great wildlife spectacles. Elk, bison, pronghorn—all have dwindled. I wondered if preserves like Lake Clark will perpetuate the glory of the caribou, which need so much room.

Days later, resting atop a granite tor, we drank in another superlative scene—half a dozen giant peaks buttressed with volcanic walls that rose more than 4,000 feet around us. Hanging glaciers supported snowfields higher up on huge corbelings of ice.

A faint, distant droning signaled the approach of an airplane, almost invisible in the grandness before us. It seemed like a mosquito in church. This abrupt reminder of the civilization to which we would so soon return sparked a flurry of remarks and reflections on the past fortnight's shared experiences:

"It's the remoteness, there's little left like it."

"And there's the element of danger, the chance that the wilderness can take you."

"I've liked even the alders. They're part of it all. Remove them and it's different—not right."

"Yes, it's the variety, the variety of environments. That's what I'll remember best."

That variety is perhaps best known and most appreciated by Dick Proenneke, who had stopped by our Twin Lakes camp while out on one of his 15-hour, 30-mile wilderness strolls.

"Come back, John, and I'll take you to see some of Twin Lakes' special treats," he invited. I accepted eagerly, and returned when autumn was painting the tundra.

Dick himself had come to see 11 years before. A former heavy-equipment operator and mechanic nearly blinded by a work accident, Dick vowed, when recovered, to miss no more of earth's natural beauty. Friends invited him to Twin Lakes, where he later built a cabin with unusual care and craftsmanship. He has since spent most of his time at the lakes, hiking, climbing, canoeing, exploring, watching and photographing the wildlife. He keeps a detailed journal and corresponds with the many friends who welcome a Twin Lakes dateline. A book about it all, *One Man's Wilderness,* has become an Alaskan classic. Said Dick: "When farmers back in my home state of Iowa say, 'You can't eat scenery,' I reply, 'but it certainly makes good seasoning for beans.'"

Having prepared two "sticks of dynamite"—rolled-up sourdough flapjacks filled with peanut butter and honey—to sustain us on our journey, Dick showed me that the Lake Clark area is as varied in detail as it is overall. Crumblings of pink rocks sugared the mountainsides above us as we hiked canyons amid the stark beauty of what Dick calls the "volcanic mountains." Through forest and glade, pausing here and there to sample juicy blueberries, we climbed to a waterfall and found a nest of moss that water ouzels had built against the waterworn rocks.

In a high cirque, crested with spires, marmots sunned. Their smaller cousins, the arctic ground squirrels, had made a clear trail through the tundra. "When squirrels can do that, I guess it tells how fragile this vegetation is," Dick commented. Later he showed me a boulder so delicately balanced on a ledge that a push with the hand could set it rocking. Borne here and dropped by some now-disappeared glacier, the rock marked the greatest height reached by that icy tongue, Dick explained. It lay halfway up the valley wall.

For Dick, every niche of Twin Lakes holds special significance:

"Over there's where the ewes lamb. They stay several days under that high cliff, then bring their lambs down to join the rest of the band."

"A moose had twin calves in the swale near the fox dens. She was one of my 'tame' cows, so I got good pictures. A moose rutting-ground is across the lake in those poplars."

"Right here on the shore a bear once popped out of the brush in front of my canoe. He was as surprised as I, and went running up the mountain."

"Bears are strange people," Dick added, showing me a tree rubbed against and clawed and bitten by a bear. The scar was seven feet above the ground. "This is their social register. If you could read bear language, this might say, 'To whom it may concern: I'm not just an ordinary bear!'"

"The best hibernation den I've come across was on the side of that mountain. It was nine feet deep, and what a view from the entrance! Over across there was the den where the sow had triplets. The cubs didn't want to leave the den, so mother packed one away by its hind leg. You know, a bear is a wise old mother. If human mothers followed bears' example, there'd be fewer spoiled kids."

Dick takes special pleasure in stalking and photographing the Dall rams in their high seclusion. "I think it hurts their pride to realize they've been sneaked up on," he said with a grin.

From cabin door or mountaintop, Dick savors each month's personality, happenings, comings and goings of fellow creatures, and the ebb and flow of life. As we watched a beaver bringing in winter groceries, I asked what would happen next. "In October the bears go in," he said. "The rams come down, the swans go by, flying south." That month, his journal bore the entry, "You guys go if you want to. Go to civilization. I'll stay a while."

He stays to watch winter come in. The sun fails to rise above his mountains after November 7. The horned grebe is the last migrant to leave, and the lakes freeze about Thanksgiving. By December, ice curtains the falls; hares and ptarmigan have donned winter fur and plumage of spotless white, and wolverine and wolf are abroad. Snow is the diary in which life writes its script of footprints. January is sunless, but in February the sun comes back from behind the peaks. By March, caribou begin returning from lower country. Lynx are squalling. Moose, feeling the pinch of winter, peel bark for food. Red squirrels begin packing dead grass for nests.

In April, the bears emerge from their dens and ground squirrels pop out of their burrows, a fact well known by the eagles that have returned to hunt them. Water drips from south-sunny banks in May, and avalanches rumble. By June the lake ice begins to squeak, then breaks up in slender crystalline "candles" that sweep before the winds and currents. June is a busy time. As soon as there is open water, the arctic terns appear, back from far Antarctica, and ptarmigan parade their chicks. The big rams leave the ewes and head for high country. Moose calve as the willows leaf out. By now the south slopes are clear of snow. Flowers—among them the purple mountain saxifrage—follow the retreating snow line in their blooming.

As June is abustle, so July is quiescent. Few animals are in evidence, save for the fox pups playing. But by August, moose and caribou appear with antlers grown in velvet, and salmon surge upriver to spawn. As blueberries ripen, the wild red currant's leaf is first to color in autumn.

Though a few lavender harebells still bloomed bravely, autumn was well on its way when Dick and I followed the caribou trail along the canyonside behind his cabin. I felt as if I were ankle-deep in rubies, so brilliant were the red alpine bearberry leaves. Snow powdered the craggy summits that soar above the lakes. It was time for me to go, though Dick would stay, as he had in years past. "Mountains are a man's best friends if he only knew it," he advised me. "You hike and climb every day and you don't grow old." I marveled at this tireless 63-year-old. Though I couldn't keep up with him, I had experienced his exhilaration and reverence for wild beauty that I hope the years will not dim. This park is for the ages, I remembered. Here generations will find and keep their youth, their love of earth.

Here, as elsewhere, care as well as vigor must be exercised. On the cabin wall above his bunk Dick has penned this question: "Is it proper that the wilderness and its creatures should suffer because we came?"

In hope and with respect, I believe that we in this great land can gently answer, "No."

Part-time prospector Harry Baker splits his time between an Anchorage home and this cabin on Lake Clark. "The clean fresh air, the sunshine and quiet solitude" drew him to the area, where he has worked a mining claim since the late thirties. He recently cut a hundred house logs and plans, at age 66, to build a new cabin.

Call of the wilderness repeatedly lured Dick Proenneke to Alaska from his native Iowa, eventually convincing him to stay. He now lives a Walden-like existence north of Lake Clark at Twin Lakes, where no road leads in or out, and only animals provide companionship throughout the year. Daily routines include hauling water (below) from the nearby lake, photographing moose (right) and other wildlife, and spoiling resident gray jays—also called camp robbers—with leftover flapjacks. Working alone with common hand tools and uncommon craftsmanship, Dick built and furnished his Twin Lakes cabin almost entirely from the surrounding forest. White spruce logs, painstakingly felled, peeled, and notched, make up the walls and roof poles. The Dutch-style front door rides on hinges he carved from spruce knees. A latch keeps out squirrels whenever Dick goes out to pick wild blueberries or to make solitary hikes about his private neighborhood.

Craggy spine of Lake Clark country, the Chigmit Mountains (above) deserve their nickname: Alaska's Alps. They isolate inland regions from the populated Cook Inlet area. So rarely has man crossed them that most features remain nameless; exceptions include Upper Twin Lake (far left) and the granite needle at left called The Tusk.

"All I really wanted to do was have a little more room, hunt and trap, and more or less cut loose," explains Bob Tracey, who left California at age 19 for Lake Clark. He became a full-time trapper, learning from Indians how to build sleds and to mush dogs. He now maintains one of the area's few working teams. As a three-year-old howls, Bob harnesses the dogs (left), then strikes out through newfallen snow to check his trapline along the brush-lined Kijik River (below). Although snowmobiles have almost totally replaced dogsleds throughout the Lake Clark region, Bob finds this more traditional method of winter travel quieter and less likely to break down. He and his dogs have covered as much as 80 miles a day. "The trapping is fairly good, and there's always a moose to be had. On the whole it's a rather nice life-style," he adds, showing off part of the season's take—a mixed armload of wolverine, red fox, and grayish lynx pelts.

Contributors

A major in art history and an interest in nature led Minnesotan JIM BRANDENBURG to photography. He became a contract photographer for the National Geographic Society in 1979. Jim contributed to the new publication *Wild Animals of North America* and has worked on several subjects for the GEOGRAPHIC—including bamboo, the Canadian Rockies, and the Badlands of South Dakota.

CONSTANCE BROWN received her degree in English literature from the University of Colorado. She worked as a journalist on the East Coast, then returned to her native Colorado in 1972, where she makes her home in Aspen. She has written on natural history, the environment, wilderness sports, and travel, and will complete a naturalist's guide to the southern Rockies in 1981.

Photographs by PAUL CHESLEY have appeared in *Geo, National Wildlife,* and *Smithsonian* magazines, and in Time-Life books. Assignments have taken him throughout the United States and to South America and Japan. Paul attended universities in the West and in Minnesota and now lives in Aspen. A Special Publication on the Continental Divide, photographed by Paul, will appear in 1981.

MARK GODFREY first worked as a photographer for the *Arizona Daily Star.* He was later on the staff of newspapers in Houston and Topeka and covered the war in Viet Nam for the Associated Press. Mark then spent several more years in Asia as a contract photographer for *Life* magazine. He lives in Arlington, Virginia, and is a member of Magnum Photos, Inc.

Free-lance photographer ANNIE GRIFFITHS took up photography at age 21, when she studied photojournalism at the University of Minnesota. She now lives in Minneapolis. *America's Magnificent Mountains,* a Special Publication that will appear in 1980, will include a chapter on the Colorado Rockies photographed by Annie.

A writer and National Park Service planner for 25 years—the last six in Alaska—JOHN KAUFFMANN has contributed to NATIONAL GEOGRAPHIC and numerous Dept. of the Interior publications. He is the author of *Flow East: A Look at Our North Atlantic Rivers.* John divides his time among Maryland, Alaska, and Maine, where he is contributing editor of the *Bar Harbor Times.*

CHRISTINE ECKSTROM LEE received her bachelor's degree in English from Mount Holyoke College in Massachusetts and joined the Society's staff in 1974. She has contributed picture legends to several Special Publications and a chapter on the Minoan civilization to *Mysteries of the Ancient World.* Her chapter on the Virgin Islands will appear in *Isles of the Caribbean* in 1980.

YVA MOMATIUK and JOHN EASTCOTT, a nomadic wife-and-husband team, feel drawn to remote parts of the world. Born and educated in Warsaw, Poland, Yva holds a degree in architecture; John, a New Zealander, received his degree in photographic arts in London. Journeys to the Arctic resulted in a book—*Great Slave Lake Blues*—for a Canadian publisher, and "Still Eskimo, Still Free: The Inuit of Umingmaktok" for the November 1977 NATIONAL GEOGRAPHIC. Yva and John received the Pacific Area Travel Association Award for Excellence for "New Zealand's High Country" in the August 1978 GEOGRAPHIC, and they have recently finished *High Country* for a New Zealand publisher. Their photographs have also appeared in *Wild Places* and *The Wild Shores of North America.*

City-bred CYNTHIA RUSS RAMSAY has explored diverse U. S. wilderness regions for recent Special Publications: the Southwest for *Into the Wilderness,* and the far north for *Alaska.* An upcoming volume, *America's Magnificent Mountains,* will include a chapter by Cynthia. She has also served as managing editor of Books for Young Explorers (for children 4 through 8).

DEAN REBUFFONI grew up in Pekin, Illinois, and earned bachelor's degrees in journalism and political science at Southern Illinois University. He has worked as a reporter for the *St. Louis Globe-Democrat* and now lives in Minneapolis, where he is environmental reporter for the *Minneapolis Tribune.* The north-woods chapter is his first assignment for the National Geographic Society.

Library of Congress ⒞ⒾⓅ Data

National Geographic Society, Washington, D. C.
   Special Publications Division.
   Exploring America's backcountry.
   Bibliography: p.
   Includes index.
   1. United States—Description and travel—1960-
—Addresses, essays, lectures.   I. Title.
E169.02.N37 1979   917.3'04   78-61265
ISBN 0-87044-273-2

JIM BRANDENBURG

CANOEISTS PORTAGE TO A PUT-IN POINT ON MOOSE LAKE IN THE BOUNDARY WATERS CANOE AREA WILDERNESS. HARDCOVER DESIGN: TINY SPRING PEEPER, A TREE FROG LESS THAN AN INCH LONG, PERCHES ON A MUSHROOM.

Additional Reading

The reader may wish to consult the *National Geographic Index* for related articles, and to refer to the following: Carlos Baker, *Ernest Hemingway;* William D. Clark, *Death Valley;* Malcolm L. Comeaux, *Atchafalaya Swamp Life: Settlement and Folk Occupations;* Dick d'Easum, *Sawtooth Tales;* Alfred L. Donaldson, *A History of the Adirondacks,* 2 vols.; Willis Frederick Dunbar, *Michigan;* Roxana S. Ferris, *Death Valley Wildflowers;* Frank Graham, Jr., *The Adirondack Park;* Charles B. Hunt, *Death Valley;* Sam Keith and Richard Proenneke, *One Man's Wilderness;* Buddy Mays, *Wildwaters: Exploring Wilderness Waterways;* and William Chapman White, *Adirondack Country.*

Acknowledgments

The Special Publications Division is grateful to the individuals, organizations, and agencies named or quoted in the text and to those cited here for their generous cooperation and assistance during the preparation of this book: David Balbough, Burton V. Barnes, Clair A. Brown, Sandra J. Brown, Malcolm L. Comeaux, Mary DeDecker, Theodore R. Dudley, Joey Dykes, Douglass Henderson, Charles B. Hunt, Victor Lambou, David O. Lee, John Lynch, Maynard M. Miller, Thomas R. Monroe, Vincent J. Moore, Milton B. Newton, Storrs L. Olson, Charles H. Racine, Bruce L. Reed, Henry W. Setzer, Stanwyn G. Shetler, Forest Stearns, Larry Underwood, Frank C. Vasek, William K. Verner, George E. Watson, Merle Wells, Al Wolter, and Lauren A. Wright; Adirondack Park Agency, Death Valley National Monument, and New York State Department of Environmental Conservation.

Index

Composition for EXPLORING AMERICA'S BACKCOUNTRY by National Geographic's Photographic Services, Carl M. Shrader, Chief; Lawrence F. Ludwig, Assistant Chief. Printed and bound by Holladay-Tyler Printing Corp., Rockville, Md. Color separations by the Lanman Companies, Washington, D. C.; Graphic South, Charlotte, N.C.; National Bickford Graphics, Inc., Providence, R.I.; Progressive Color Corp., Rockville, Md.; The J. Wm. Reed Co., Alexandria, Va.